MIGUEL DELIBES

by

Janet W. Díaz

This is the first published critical study in English of Miguel Delibes, who has been the subject of many articles and unpublished theses in Spanish, English and other languages. One of Spain's leading novelists of the post-war era, Delibes is seen in the triple dimension of educator, journalist and narrator, with his works projected against the background of recent history. The author investigates Delibes' short stories and novels from several angles, relating them to the novelist's total personality, his vital experiences or contemporary circumstances, aspects of his philosophy, or to the artistic evolution of Delibes. While each work is analyzed as an entity in itself, it is also placed in the perspective of Delibes' production to date, utilizing an eclectic critical approach. Delibes emerges as a complex writer, still dynamically evolving. Far from being simply the sardonic painter of rural Castile revealed in his best-known works, he is an increasingly sophisticated novelist whose latest publications clearly reflect growing aesthetic concerns. Delibes' life and writings are seen against the background of Valladolid, in particular, and contemporary Spain, in general, with his work placed in relation to present and preceding Spanish literature.

TWAYNE'S WORLD AUTHORS SERIES (TWAS)

The purpose of TWAS is to survey the major writers—novelists, dramatists, historians, poets, philosophers, and critics—of the nations of the world. Among the national literatures covered are those of Australia, Canada, China, Eastern Europe, France, Germany, Greece, India, Italy, Japan, Latin America, the Netherlands, New Zealand, Poland, Russia, Scandinavia, Spain, and the African nations, as well as Hebrew, Yiddish, and Latin Classical literatures. This survey is complemented by Twayne's United States Authors Series and English Authors Series.

The intent of each volume in these series is to present a critical-analytical study of the works of the writer; to include biographical and historical material that may be necessary for understanding, appreciation, and critical appraisal of the writer; and to present all material in clear, concise English—but not to vitiate the scholarly content of the work by doing so.

Miguel Delibes

BY JANET DIAZ

University of North Carolina

ABOUT THE AUTHOR

Janet Winecoff Díaz holds the A.B.
in Foreign Languages from the University of Missouri (Kansas City), and
the M.A. and Ph.D. in Romance Languages from Duke University. She
presently teaches Spanish at the University of North Carolina. Her specialization is the twentieth century, with
emphasis on the post-war Spanish
novel, poetry, drama and philosophy.
She has numerous critical articles on
these genres, and is the author of
*The Major Themes of Existentialism
in the Works of Ortega y Gasset,* as
well as of a study of *Ana María
Matute* (in the Twayne series).

lew York

To David

Preface

The purpose of this book is to introduce to a general public whose primary language is English the personality and writings of one of Spain's most important narrators in the period following the Civil War of 1936–1939. Because certain aspects of life and culture in Spain are not well known outside the peninsula, some explanations have been given, this in order to facilitate the understanding of the writer and his works. Delibes is by professional training a specialist in commerce, and thus it is natural that economic problems acquire a notable importance in his writing. However, Delibes does not approach Spain's social and economic inequities in the same spirit as many of his contemporaries, cultivators of the so-called social novel, and an attempt has been made in this study to distinguish between his perspective and treatment of this problematic situation and its handling by a majority of other Spanish novelists in the past two decades. Rather than drawing comparisons with specific writers or works, the distinctions made are between Delibes and the general tenets and tendencies of the movement. This accounts for the proportion of attention accorded economic and social factors in what is primarily a literary study.

Contrary to the usual practice of Spain's professional writers who tend to establish their residence in one of the literary centers, Madrid or Barcelona, and in whose lives an important part is played by *tertulias* (regular literary gatherings and discussions), Delibes has remained in relative isolation in his native Valladolid. He is less influenced by novelistic movements and fads, and is therefore a more independent writer, both by reason of his freely chosen solitude and his temperament, although his work does reflect the predominant concerns of contemporary writers within Spain. The preoccupation for the problems of man in the twentieth century, characteristic of literatures in nearly all of Occidental culture, lies at the very core of his novels, so that he is by no means out of touch with the important ideas of the day. Delibes' residence in Valladolid is significant for another reason, since this provincial capital and the surrounding countryside serve as the setting for almost all his narratives. His lifelong acquaintance with

Castile, the combination of love and anguish with which it inspires him, equips him to give a fresh and entirely original focus to treatments of this region. The area has constituted an important literary theme since the "Generation of 1898."

There is almost unanimous accord in placing Delibes in the forefront of living Spanish narrators, one of a triumvirate formed by Camilo José Cela, Ana María Matute, and himself. He is less known internationally than either of the other two, however, partly for political reasons (he was initially identified with the supporters of the Franco regime, and was apparently conservative in his early writings). This caused something close to ostracism from more liberal literary circles. While his outspoken opposition to many governmental policies during the past ten to fifteen years has subsequently shown the injustice of his critics' attitude, it continues to be rather widespread, even inside Spain. Another reason for the limited diffusion of Delibes' works outside Spain is inherent in the nature of his writing: His style, often linguistically rich, is all but untranslatable because of his use of regional dialect, colloquialisms, a specialized sublanguage, and slang. This does not explain, however, the relatively small number of in-depth critical studies of his work, particularly in English, where only a handful of articles exists. Much of the investigation which has been done on Delibes is unpublished, consisting of a number of theses and dissertations, but these usually cover only his first five or six novels.

Since most of the secondary material pertaining to Delibes and his work covers only his early writings, various misconceptions exist. The novelist has evolved and changed, perhaps radically, while general opinions still tend to be based on his beginnings. Actually, his work can be divided into three fairly distinct groups: (1) the rather ponderous novels of realistic and traditional orientation, including *La sombra del ciprés es alargada* (1948), *Aún es de día* (1949), and *Mi idolatrado hijo Sisí* (1953); (2) novels of a simpler, more lyric style and anecdotal structure, lacking the formal plots of the first group, including *El camino* (1950), the interrelated *Diaries* of Lorenzo, *Diario de un cazador* (1955) and *Diario de un emigrante* (1958), some of the novelettes in the collection *Siestas con viento Sur* (1957), *La hoja roja* (1959), and *Las ratas* (1962). The third period, more experimental, is characterized by a vastly more complex syntax and a deliberate use of different techniques and structures, as well as a return to the interest in psychology found in the first novels. This last group includes the scattered short stories published after 1962 and Delibes' two most recent novels, *Cinco horas con Mario* (1966), and *Parábola del náufrago*

(1969). The third phase is still largely unapproached by the critics; prevailing ideas and opinions are based largely on the novels of the first group, plus *El camino*. Delibes' personal and literary integrity does not permit him to renounce his first attempts, although he now considers them faltering and misdirected. Because of his evolution literarily, aesthetically, philosophically, and perhaps ideologically, it is particularly important that more be known of his later writing.

The present study has included and considered at some length books by Delibes which are not fiction: his four travel books, two books on hunting, and a collection of essays. They are given inclusion here not only because of what they reveal of their author's personality and biography, but particularly because of the light they occasionally cast on more "literary" works through their direct and clear presentation of personal ideas and opinions. It is in these miscellaneous writings that Delibes reveals many of the preoccupations and motives underlying his novels, often susceptible of misinterpretation because he does not preach or overtly moralize in his fiction.

This study follows no specific critical school, and offers no thesis; it is simply an attempt to present a complete vision of Delibes as a human being and as a writer, to relate his works to his life, to the environment in which they were produced, and to interrelate his writings to each other. Emphasis has been given to constants in his work, to repeated or obsessive themes and motifs, to characteristic techniques and rhetorical devices, while at the same time an effort is made to show the novelist's evolution, to indicate the nature of change, and to suggest possible future directions by pointing out the more durable elements which have persisted despite the writer's consistent artistic progress. Some two hundred articles, reviews, books, and theses treating Delibes' work were read in the course of the research for this book, but nearly all are difficult of access, either because of their having been published in Spanish newspapers unavailable in this country, in journals of limited circulation, or because they remain unpublished.

The present writer is indebted to Miguel Delibes for his cooperation in making available his private collection of secondary material, as well as for his kindness in granting interviews and answering questions by letter. This background information, obtained for the most part in Spain, was collected before the publication of *Cinco horas con Mario* and *Parábola del náufrago,* so that there is little or no reference to criticism of these two novels. Actually, the latter is at this writing so recent that almost nothing about it has appeared. And given the nature of the novel, many Spanish critics will hesitate to touch it prior to changes in the political and intellectual climate. Many bibliographical items have been eliminated from this study as repetitive or of insufficient interest, while others which could not be fitted into the textual discussion without forcing are treated in the annotated bibliography.

Translations, which are kept to a minimum, are mine. Because of the difficulties, already mentioned, of doing justice to Delibes in translation, it was felt that a better idea of the nature and flavor of his work could be given by paraphrasing, by more lengthy description and summary, or through more extensive analysis. Most of the direct quotations from Delibes come from writings revealing his literary and philosophical ideas, rather than from his narratives themselves, but this is a necessity imposed by the character of Delibes' fiction and the belief that it is better to convey the essential content and atmosphere rather than a mutilation of the Spanish text. It is hoped that this study will serve as an introduction to the "complete Delibes" for scholars on a variety of levels, that it will modify certain opinions about him now outdated by his evolution as a writer, and that it may stimulate more detailed investigation of a first-rate novelist who has yet to receive the attention he deserves.

Janet Díaz

University of North Carolina
at Chapel Hill

Contents

Chronology

1957   *Siestas con viento Sur* (*Siestas with the Southern Breeze* [novelettes]) published. Delibes travels, lectures in Portugal.

1958   Publication of *Diario de un emigrante (An Emigrant's Diary)*. Delibes becomes Director of *El norte de Castilla*.

1959   *La hoja roja (The Red Leaf)* published.

1960   Travels in Germany.

1961   Publishes *Por esos mundos* (*Round About the World* [travel]).

1962   *Las ratas (The Rats)* published in January.

1963   *Las ratas* obtains Critics' Prize. Publication of *La caza de la perdiz roja (Hunting the Red Partridge)* and *Europa, parada y fonda* (*Europe, Stops and Inns* [travel]). Delibes forced to resign directorship of *El norte de Castilla* in May.

1964   Publication of *El libro de la caza menor (Small Game Hunting)*; also of *Viejas historias de Castilla la Vieja* (*Old Tales of Old Castile* [novelette]). Delibes travels to United States in fall as Visiting Professor at University of Maryland.

1965   Lectures at numerous American Universities.

1966   *USA y yo* [*USA and I* [travel]) published; also *Cinco horas con Mario (Five Hours with Mario)*.

1968   Publication of *Vivir al día* (*Living from Day to Day* [articles]). Delibes visits Czechoslovakia. *La primavera de Praga* (*Springtime in Prague* [travel]) published.

1969   Publication of *Parábola del náufrago (Parable of the Drowning Man)*.

1970   *La mortaja (The Shroud)* published, containing varied short stories. Publishes *Con la escopeta al hombro (Shouldering the Gun)*, hunting and related memoirs. Delibes at work on antiwar novel.

CHAPTER 1

Origins of a Novelist

I *Childhood*

MIGUEL DELIBES Setién was born in the provincial capital of Valladolid, in northern Castile, the 17th of October, 1920. The third of eight children, he was raised in a conservative, middle-class family which emphasized the home and domestic life, religion, and morality. His father, Alonso Delibes Cortés, a lawyer originally from Santander, held for many years a professorship of Mercantile Law in the Valladolid School of Commerce, a position in which Miguel would eventually replace him. His mother, María Setién, was a native of Burgos. The Delibes-Setién family was a model of normal felicity, a factor which undoubtedly determined the importance of the family institution in the future novelist's work.

Those familiar with Iberian patronymics will suspect that the name Delibes is not originally Spanish, and some may associate it with the French musical composer, an uncle of Delibes' grandfather. The latter, Frederic-Pierre Delibes, an engineer, came to Spain to direct the construction of the railroad from Reinosa to Santander and to supervise the drilling of a tunnel in the village of Molledo-Portolín, between Reinosa and Torrelavega, where he met and married Saturnina Cortés. They settled permanently in Spain.

The grandmother's village, often visited by his family when Delibes was a boy, served as a model for the hamlet portrayed in *El camino (The Path),*[1] one of his most successful novels. This area, as the novelist has noted, is included by geographers as part of Old Castile, but is entirely different from what is usually considered typical Castilian topography. Located for the most part in the Cantabrian Mountains, the region is called "La Montaña," "The Mountains," although it is no more mountainous than various other parts of Castile. Its fifty miles of coastline with Santander in the center are Castile's only access to the sea, and the landscape recalls Switzerland more than the Castilian plateau, with its streams and rivers, chalet-type houses and wooden balconies, lush fields, and prosperous cows; it is quite unlike the barren, dusty villages and khaki-colored land around Valladolid, which are portrayed in so many of Delibes' works. "La Montaña" was also the setting for some of the best-known narratives of the nineteenth-century regional novelist, José María de Pereda, with whom Delibes has been compared,[2] but the resemblances are fairly superficial, as the comtemporary writer himself has stated.

"La Montaña" is squeezed between the Basque provinces on the east and the onetime kingdom of Asturias to the west, and many of its cultural traits—games, folklore, customs, and Visigothic architecture—owe more to these neighbors than to Castile. Perhaps it was partly for these reasons that Delibes, Castilian novelist par excellence, subsequently chose to exclude the *montaña* from further appearances in his work, despite the overwhelming success of *The Path.*

The boyhood of the future novelist was largely uneventful, and only a few minor incidents have been recorded: at the age of four, he one day lost his way and wandered about the city until picked up by the municipal police. His first schooling, comparable to the kindergarten level, was with the Carmelite nuns in the Campo Grande section of Valladolid, not far from the Delibes home, and like many a normal boy of his age, Miguel fell in love with his teacher, Mother Luciana. At seven, he began to attend the Colegio de Lourdes, a private school operated by the Christian Brothers, where he would later received his only lessons in literature with Brother José María; he proved to be a quite average student in this area of study.

The political unrest of the years 1930–1936 was acutely felt in Valladolid, a center of conservative activity. Boys from Delibes' school had frequent unpleasant encounters with street urchins, from whom they had to defend their lunches, but except for this, Miguel's life continued to be tranquil and perhaps rather dull. He was a soccer enthusiast, playing forward center on his class team, and his literary aspirations in this period were limited to a few zealous reports of their games. From childhood, he showed unusual curiosity for animals and nature, tending to be empirical in his investigations. Intrigued, for example, by the problem of whether mice could swim, he filled a bathtub and threw one in.[3] He also attempted to raise newly-hatched wild birds, perhaps as a result of his interest in hunting. His father, a dedicated hunter, gave the boy an early initiation in this sport, which would become his passionate, lifelong avocation, as well as the subject of novels, short stories, and a number of more technical treatments. At the age of eleven, he received his first bird gun, and for many years carried his father's game bag. From the age of four, he lived surrounded by guns and ammunition, knapsacks, dogs, and the other trappings of the hunt, and each Saturday would assist his father in the preparations for the predawn sally on Sundays. Delibes asserts somewhat humorously in the prologue to the second volume of his *Complete Works* that because of his extreme youth, he was unaware that other distractions existed; and because his father was a serious man who became emotionally aroused only while discussing hunting and politics, he deduced that the former was at least as important as the latter, and certainly much more so than one's profession. To judge from the anecdotes he adduces in this connection, it does seem that the only interruptions of general domestic tranquility were motivated by mishaps related to the hunt or hunting gear.

The relationship with his father was particularly important in the future novelist's formative years, as might well be deduced from external data such as his having elected the same profession and hobby. Their closeness, however, seems to have had at least one long-term negative effect. Delibes' father was rather elderly, or imagined to be so by the boy; he recalls him as always white-haired, and for many years was haunted by the fear and dread of his father's death. The obsessive theme of death in his works, noticed by many critics, is conjectured by Delibes to be an outgrowth of this preoccupation of his childhood. He also attributes to this long anxiety a tendency to occasional pessimism and psychic depression. Another probable direct result is the frequency and importance of the parent-child relationship in Delibes' writings, a capital factor whether portrayed favorably or unfavorably. The father-son relationship especially is stressed in several works, notably the long thesis novel *Mi idolatrado hijo Sisí (My Adored Son Sisí)*, the novelettes *Los nogales (The Walnut Trees)* and *La mortaja (The Shroud);* and its absence is a significant psychological determinant in his first novel, *La sombra del ciprés es alargada (Long Is the Cypress' Shadow)*, where motivation centers upon the obsessive fear of losing a loved one.

The boy Delibes especially enjoyed the summers, when his family would move to a house belonging to his grandparents in Molledo-Portolín. The contrast between this mountain village and Valladolid may have well been his first inkling of the city's negative potential for childhood, its ability to constrain and oppress, compared with the freedom of field and forest. This could quite likely have originated the city-country duality which often appears in Delibes' work: the city as focus of an overwhelmingly negative advance of "progress," civilization in its least desirable aspects, counterbalanced by a slightly idealized portrait of nature, with its healing virtues, the last refuge of individualism in a mass society. However, Delibes is too well acquainted with the brutality and primitivism of life in Castile's villages and countryside to idealize all that is not the city. He treats rural areas and their inhabitants with a tenderness born partly of pity inspired by the miserable, ruinous villages and desolate, exhausted fields, and partly because of his love of nature, which became a passion during the youthful hunting trips with his father. He mentions also that his favorite readings of early years were related to the landscape, nature, and the hunt, listing the works of Zane Grey, James Curwood, and Salgari. On the other hand, Jules Verne upset and disturbed him, a fact which the mature novelist relates to what he calls "cosmic terror, vertigo, and moderate claustrophobia."[4]

Valladolid is not a large city, and in another country might be considered only a big town. Presently an important rail center of some two hundred thousand, it is suffering growing pains. The proportionately great increase in size of the past few years is due mostly to postwar industrialization and emigration from impoverished rural areas to the cities. Valladolid is not ancient, but rather new by Spanish standards, probably not having completed its first millennium. Actually the truth of its founding is probably forever lost, although one version holds that it was founded by a Moor called Olid, receiving from its founder the name of "Valle de Olid," which subsequently degenerated to the present pronunciation and spelling. This version is questionable both historically and linguistically, and probably owes as much to fantasy as to fact. In any case, if Valladolid was founded by the Moors, no traces of these origins remain. It is more likely that its beginnings date from the period of the Reconquest, either in the eleventh or early twelfth century, when this section of Castile was recaptured from the Moorish occupants. One article by Delibes states that the founder of the city was Count Ansúrez, but he gives no further details.

The city is rather unimportant from the artistic standpoint, although somewhat more significant historically. It was twice the capital of Spain (in a period when the location of the capital depended upon the residence of the king), and most of its notable buildings are mansions of the early Renaissance, a bit overoptimistically denominated "palaces": The Palacio de los Vivero, where Ferdinand and Isabel were married; another nearby where Philip II was born; and a house which reputedly belonged to Columbus. It was in Valladolid in 1506 that the discoverer of America died, and was provisionally buried in the monastery of Cuevas de Itálica until his remains were transported to Santo Domingo. Most events of historical importance which transpired in Valladolid date from the fifteenth and sixteenth centuries: the execution of Don Alvaro de Luna, favorite of the King Don Juan II, in 1453, celebrated in many works of Spanish literature; and in the following century, the famous *autos de fe*, "acts of faith," of the Inquisition. Valladolid was briefly a center of Lutheranism, stamped out by Philip II, who allegedly inaugurated his reign by attending two *autos de fe* in Valladolid in 1559. It is reported that when one of the condemned appealed to him for mercy, the monarch replied: "If my son were a heretic like you, I would carry the wood to burn him myself." Another source states that on this occasion, sixty-one persons were condemned, twenty-seven of them to be burned alive, two in effigy (having escaped), and the rest to various penances.[5] Whether because of these grisly antecedents or some innate conservatism, Valladolid soon after settled into a sleepy lethargy, unbroken for centuries by events of any transcendent historical or cultural significance.

Up to the time of the Spanish Civil War, the city was largely an agrarian center, with a thoroughly provincial and stagnant cultural life, and a static socio-economic growth pattern. There are few monuments there to attract the traveler: although it has many churches, none are of special interest. Its cathedral, still unfinished, is solid, cold, and austere, in the style of Herrera, architect of the Escorial. There is a small university, where Delibes was examined for one of his degrees, but was never a student. Also located in Valladolid is the National Museum of Polychrome Sculpture, a peculiarly Spanish religious art form. The most important artist represented is Berruguete; many works are anonymous or by little-known sculptors, but the collection is unique in the world: images in wood, vividly painted and sometimes horribly realistic, with their reproduction of open sores, wounds, blood, and tears, an art both terrible and genuinely Spanish, albeit a minor form, little known beyond the bounds of Castile. That Valladolid should have been in a sense the center of this artistic activity perhaps illuminates something of the area's historic mentality.

In modern times, one of the city's major attractions is its celebration of Holy Week, in typical Spanish style, with the participation of members of the various *cofradías* or lay brotherhoods, their hoods and pointed hats recalling the past associations with the Inquisition. Many buildings still have their iron balconies with candelabra where tapers are placed in Holy Week to light the streets through which the procession passes, narrow, tortuous streets utterly lacking in symmetry, and lined by ancient houses with few windows, their arched doorways lit by feeble lanterns and protected by a cross. The Plaza Mayor (Main Square) is surrounded by buildings whose ground floors form an arcade, filled with small businesses: tailors, hatmakers, and bookstores which sell mostly stationery items, as the local population is not overly given to reading. There are also cafés, usually full of domino players, and a movie theater which shows American films. The area at the *paseo* hour throngs with priests and men in military uniform, who seem even more abundant in Valladolid than in other parts of Spain. The most important plaza in the new part of the city is that of the poet Zorrilla, a famous Romantic playwright, one of the few native sons of Valladolid to achieve national cultural renown. In the twentieth century, the city produced another great literary figure in the person of the poet, Jorge Guillén.

Located in the steppe-like, frequently waterless tablelands of northern Castile, Valladolid has a severe climate, which even its own Chamber of Commerce describes as "harsh in winter and summer." Agriculture is still important, and much of the city's new industrial activity, such as artificial fertilizer production, is related to the area's basically agrarian orientation. The importance of agriculture is also reflected in the number of bookstores whose entire display window is devoted to agricultural treatises, and the space devoted to agrarian affairs in the pages of *El norte de Castilla,* the second oldest daily newspaper in Spain. It is not surprising, therefore, that agriculture, the flat, rocky land, and cruel Castilian climate loom so large in Delibes' writings.

The city is something of a minor cultural center, with such activities mainly in the Ateneo and the offices of *El norte* .... These two institutions attempt to keep the residents of Valladolid and surrounding areas in touch with what is happening in the rest of Spain, and to a lesser extent, the world at large. This is not an easy task, for despite recent industrialization and expansion, poverty is still very much in evidence, with an enormous number of beggars (proportionately far more than in Madrid or Barcelona), and many narrow, dirty, ruinous streets, their crumbling buildings often juxtaposed haphazardly with new constructions. Delibes has portrayed this decaying section of Valladolid in *Aún es de día (Still It Is Day)*, his second novel, and other areas of the city serve as settings for many other narratives.

II *Adolescence*

Delibes early showed remarkable energy, a willingness to carry on several simultaneous activities, which goes back to his school days. At the time he attended the Colegio de Lourdes, he was also matriculated in the Instituto Zorrilla (on the high school level, but public). In the latter, an end-of-year review, similar to high school and college yearbooks, described the adolescent Miguel as "of languid gaze and a little sad, but nevertheless, the most high-spirited and playful."[6] Delibes has described himself as a timid, withdrawn boy who enjoyed the human warmth and affection of his home, and whose attachment to his parents led to extremes of anguish and anxiety. These same traits can be distinghished in many of his youthful protagonists, particularly those of the early works. Miguel was a devout boy, and suffered pangs of conscience because of his lack of religious vocation, worrying over the possibility that God might call and he would fail to hear. While this exaggerated scrupulousness was eventually outgrown, he continued to retain his steadfast faith.

Upon the outbreak of the Spanish Civil War in July of 1936, Delibes, who was still not sixteen, was too young for military service. He had finished his *bachillerato* (roughly the equivalent of a high school diploma) shortly before, but was unable to enroll in the University as it was closed throughout the conflict. He therefore whiled away his time taking classes in the School of Commerce, an accident of fate which may have been decisive in his choice of career. At the same time, he took night classes in modeling and sculpture, perhaps an indication of his burgeoning talent and need for artistic expression which had not yet found the means of self-realization. He had previously become known among his secondary-school classmates for his sketches, a form which he continued to cultivate after abandoning the other excursion into art. His night classes clashed with his interest in the movies, which eventually triumphed in the competing timetable.

Later in the war, having reached the age when he could serve as a volunteer, Delibes enlisted in the Nationalist (Franco) navy, and saw brief service on the cruiser *"Canarias,"* whose assignment was coastal patrol and blockade. His contact with war as such was limited, and the one transcendent incident occurred when his ship participated in rescue operations after a tourist vessel was torpedoed by a German submarine. This experience is reflected literarily in an adventure of Pedro, protagonist of *Long Is the Cypress' Shadow*. Delibes never really saw the enemy; he observed only war's innocent victims, but this produced in him a lasting aversion to war, whatever its causes, and once the civil conflict ended, he became a determined nonpartisan, often opposing the government he had originally helped to bring to power, and doing everything within his means to assist former opponents, the Republican political prisoners. Unselfishly, he took a good many risks to help these people as they were released from the several jails located in Valladolid and vicinity.

At the close of hostilities, Delibes considered making a career in the navy (even though he now says the sea was depressing for him), but a slight defect in his vision excluded this possibility. Therefore, from 1939 to 1941, he took advantage of intensive courses offered at the war's end to finish the equivalent of two university-level degrees in law and commerce, but because of the nature of his studies, affirms that he had "no alma mater." His next career move was to obtain a position in the Banco Castellano (Bank of Castile), seeking practical, inside knowledge of financial operations as an adjunct to his further preparation for teaching Mercantile Law. His first salary in this position was 189 pesetas per month,[7] less than three dollars at the present exchange, although substantially more favorable rates prevailed then. However, in the disastrous economy of postwar Spain, with almost all items in short supply and sold at black-market prices, this was far from a living wage. After some six months, Delibes returned to his studies, preparing for the examinations for the degree of "Intendencia Mercantil," a doctorate in commerce.

Until it became necessary to prepare his doctoral thesis, Delibes had never seriously faced the problems of written self-expression, and his literary interests had been practically nonexistent. It is now something of a habit for him to assert that "Don Joaquín Garrigues' course in Mercantile Law led me to literature."[8] He is not being paradoxical; his praise for this professor's text indicates that in reading what otherwise must have been somewhat dull, technical material, he first became aware of certain difficulties of expression and different means of resolving them. Delibes' doctoral thesis was entitled "Causes of Dissolution of Corporations."[9] According to the novelist, his specific investigations were of the ceramics industry, its organization, production, and markets.[10]

During the same period that he spent in the Banco Castellano, Delibes had also begun his long association with the newspaper, *El norte de Castilla*, working initially as a caricaturist at a salary of one hundred pesetas monthly. This employment obviously grew out of his youthful avocation for drawing, and at the same time anticipates his tendency to literary caricaturization, obvious in many works. He has continued illustrating on a lesser scale more recently, with sketches for the American edition of *The Path*. An exposition of his caricatures in Valladolid, held near the beginning of his professional drawing experience, was most successful. In order to earn still more, he also did Christmas cards, obviously not a typical Spanish institution, as they are still known there as "tarjetas de Christmas," without translating the name of the holiday.

Also in 1941, Delibes met his future wife, Angeles de Castro, while walking along the traditional paseo of Campo Grande, a park in the better part of the city where sweethearts were accustomed to stroll. He fell in love, and began to sign his sketches "MAX" (M=Miguel, A=Angeles, X=future). He continued study toward a doctorate in law at the same time as preparing for the "Intendencia Mercantil" and working at his two jobs, and in 1943 went to Madrid to take an intensive three-month course in journalism, during which time he also passed examinations in the courses for his doctorate of laws, but without doing the thesis. The feverish commercial and legal study formed part of a program to ready himself to undergo the "oposiciones a cátedra" (public examinations for a professorial chair), as he felt a sense of obligation to replace his father, who was retiring. Much of 1944 was spent in the preparation for these examinations, but Delibes took advantage of his recent study of journalism to broaden his work with *El norte de Castilla*, becoming a writer of editorials, movie critic, and then member of the editorial board. His critiques were often signed with a pseudonym, "Seco" or "Miguel Seco," which he has continued to use upon occasion.

Delibes was also briefly director of a poetry review, *Halcón*, apparently without being attracted by poetry himself, for he confessed to an interviewer: "Really, poetry is of little interest to me. I never wrote a verse and read very few."[11] According to the novelist, he was chosen by the aspiring poets because of being the only one in the group with the necessary journalist's card, required to direct a magazine; presumably the directorship was undertaken as a favor to his friend, the poet Manuel Alonso Alcalde.

In 1945[12] Delibes succeeded in obtaining the chair of Mercantile

Law, although whatever enthusiasm he may have had for the subject was of short duration, as he subsequently changed to other areas of teaching, occupying the chair of History of Culture in the same School of Commerce in Valladolid. In an undated autobiographical note, Delibes also mentions teaching the History of Commerce. His second area of specialization was history, and as part of his *oposiciones* Delibes was required to write an essay on "Causes of the Protestant Reformation." Perhaps this experience, combined with the doctoral thesis and journalistic activities, awakened further literary aspirations, because at approximately the same time, Delibes wrote his first short story, "La bujía" ("The Spark Plug"), submitted to a magazine contest where it won second prize. The story was not preserved, and the author recalls nothing more than the title. Delibes' training in history produced two technical volumes, probably intended for scholastic use, sometime prior to 1955. These are not included in his bibliographies, and the only notice of their existence is found in a newspaper report, attributing to him these titles: *Síntesis de historia universal (A Synthesis of Universal History)* and *Síntesis de historia de España (A Synthesis of Spanish History)*.[13]

III *Adulthood*

Delibes married his fiancée in 1946, after five years of waiting, when at last they succeeded in purchasing an apartment. With a somewhat more tranquil existence, and stimulated by his wife, Delibes began to read more widely, although not systematically. While his marriage was completely happy, he began to suffer periods of melancholy and depression, just as during his childhood and adolescence, moods temporarily mitigated by the feverish activity of preceding years. It was largely to combat this mental state that he began his first novel, although it can be presumed that his relative tranquility was also important, offering the first opportunity for mature reflections on the nature of life. In February of 1947, Delibes' first son, another Miguel, was born. One critic affirms that this boy served as model for various juvenile characters created by the novelist, in particular "el Nini" of *Las ratas (The Rats)* and the young Mario of *Cinco horas con Mario (Five Hours with Mario.*[14] No supporting evidence is adduced, but presumably the statement is based upon remarks to this effect by Delibes.

In May, some three months after the birth of his son, Delibes commenced *Long Is the Cypress' Shadow,* in which, as he has confessed, he gave novelistic expression to "an obsession which I have carried since childhood: death."[15] Apparently written in part for its cathartic effect, the novel was also written with the intention of submitting it to the contest for the Nadal Prize, then the most prestigious and highly endowed in Spain. Because of the deadline for submitting manuscripts to the Nadal judges, whose decision was to be made the 6th of January following, some of the novel (especially the last part) seems to have been done in haste. Critics have subsequently called this novel an artistic error, a mistaken path for Delibes' talents, and he himself intuited something of this before submitting it, although he went ahead with his initial plan. Despite these doubts, Delibes has often since said that if he had not won, he most likely would not have continued writing. One hundred twelve novels competed for the prize, including works by writers who would subsequently become well known, such as Rosa María Cajal and Ana María Matute, and one novelist already with an established reputation, Manuel Pombo Angulo.

The night of the judging in January of 1948, Delibes and several friends sat anxiously in the offices of *El norte* . . . . beside the teletype, which broke down while transmitting the results of the voting. By means of a telephone call to his brother, Federico, who was in Barcelona on the scene, Delibes learned that he had won. The final vote was close, with three of the five judges favoring Delibes, and two voting for *Hospital general* of Pombo Angulo. The sharp competition provoked some nasty polemics, with personal attacks upon Delibes by the backers of Pombo Angulo.[16] A good deal of the arguments appeared in the pages of *Destino,* a magazine published by the enterprise awarding the Nadal Prize, which undoubtedly stood to profit by the publicity, having published both novels in question. Despite the favorable opinions of important literary figures—the dean of living Spanish novelists, Pío Baroja; one of Spain's few Nobel Prize winners, playwright Jacinto Benavente; and other members of the Spanish Academy, distinguished critics Narciso Alonso Cortés, Melchor Fernández Almagro, and Francisco de Cossío—Delibes was deeply wounded by the attacks, which may have solidified his self-isolation from Spanish literary circles. The majority of Spanish writers eventually locate in Madrid or Barcelona, the centers of literary and artistic activity, but he has continued steadfastly in Valladolid, remaining relatively independent of narrative fashions and cliques.

The secretary of the Nadal jury, R. Vásquez-Zamora, himself a critic, made the trip from Barcelona to Valladolid to present Delibes the fifteen thousand peseta prize, and frankly declared that he had not voted for him, proceeding to explain his reasons. As it was the first constructive criticism he received, Delibes was grateful; despite having intuited defects in the novel, he lacked the criteria and experience to analyze them. He was able to put Vásquez-Zamora's observations to good use, and has ever since been his admirer.

Other reviewers believed they saw in Delibes' novel an influence of Proust, as it was comparable in being an introspective work in *tempo lento*. Actually, there was little other basis for comparison, and Delibes had had no prior acquaintance with the works of the French novelist. Although he was sufficiently intrigued by these affirmations to read some of Proust's writing, he did not proceed from this to a systematic study of literature, and years later declared to an interviewer: "I read little and in disorderly fashion. Books create problems for me rather than solving them."[17] He was not rejecting the idea of possible influence, but frankly declaring his limitations. Delibes also stated several times that he "came to literature with only the shirt on his back," and learned much from the critics.

One place where Delibes' novel was an unqualified success was in Valladolid, where citizens were wildly enthused by the honor awarded a native son. Some launched a campaign to obtain for Delibes a medal from the city, but when this was endorsed by a newspaper, *Diario Regional,* Delibes begged them to desist. A similar situation occurs in *My Adored Son Sisí* when the pompous and vacuous protagonist expects the Medal of Valladolid for a nearly useless invention. Whether Delibes was acquainted with a real, historical antecedent, or had begun to gestate parts of the future novel in his mind, the determining reason was undoubtedly his innate modesty and an unwillingness to contribute further in any way to the polemic.

Still It Is Day, published in October of 1949, shows the reaction of Delibes to the criticism of his first novel. There had been frequent objections to the atmosphere of melancholy and pessims, so the novelist created a protagonist representing almost the opposite extreme, an equally extravagant optimism, inasmuch as the attitudes of both principal characters are largely independent of their circumstances. But the novel itself is hardly optimistic, being a quasi-naturalistic description of sordid, negative, and almost hopeless conditions. Delibes has denied any naturalistic intent in writing the novel, saying that his literary formation at that time was so sketchy that he did not know what Naturalism was; his intent was to be realistic. Critics began to refer to the pair of novels in terms of opposites, *historia de un pesimismo* ("a tale of pessimism") and *historia de un optimismo* ("a tale of optimism"). However, the two works resemble each other sufficiently in their rather ponderous, rhetorical style, and philosophical, moralizing and ethical bent, despite the polarity of the protagonists, that some observers believed they could now discern "constants" in the novelist, a basis sufficient to predict the future course of his writing. As the two narratives also shared a good deal of introspection, self-questioning, and a common religious solution, further discussion ensued as to whether or not Delibes was really a "Catholic novelist." He was dismayed, in view of his devoutness, to find that some priests called into question the orthodoxy of his beliefs as reflected in his first novels.

Whether in disgust at the impossibility of pleasing them, or for whatever the reasons, Delibes began henceforth to show an increasing independence of the critics, and to experiment more with his style, simplifying and seeking his own authentic, personal tone. The fruit of this process, *The Path,* his third novel, was an unqualified success, and some critics continue to consider it his best. This short narrative was allegedly written in some twenty days during a family vacation in the summer of 1950. Less ambitious than the previous works, compact, with an almost classic simplicity, *The Path* met with instant and gratifying approval. Even though his next novel was to be in some ways a regression to the more extensive and ponderous earlier style, *The Path* exemplifies many of the best traits of Delibes and is in the same vein as those works (beginning in 1955) which are now considered his most characteristic.

During the early years of his marriage and novelistic career, Delibes devoted afternoons to his teaching and newspaper work, but had mornings mostly free to write. While suffering from a ganglion in 1951, he spent several months of involuntary leisure, fighting boredom by beginning to work on what is perhaps his most ambitious novel, *My Adored Son Sisí,* the writing of which occupied his available time for over two years. Published in 1953, this was also a success with critics and public, and seemingly marked Delibes' consecration in intellectual circles, for he subsequently began to be in demand as a lecturer. With the perspective of several years, however, there are scholars who consider this fourth long novel to be a step backward, a return to the traditionalism and solemnity, moralizing and stolidness of the first two works. But *My Adored Son Sisí* does evince further experimentation on Delibes' part, and its technique has been compared with that of Dos Passos (also unknown to Delibes) in the utilization of newspaper extracts. In documenting his study of a period beginning some ten years before his own lifetime and ending with the Civil War, Delibes relied heavily upon the archives of *El norte* . . . , easily accessible because of his continuing association with that daily.

Delibes was thus launched upon the triple career which would characterize his most active and productive years, simultaneously combining the functions of professor, newspaperman, and novelist. Although he continued to reside permanently in Valladolid, he began to travel, briefly at first, going in 1948 to the south of France and to northeast Africa in 1950. Looking back upon this period of his life, the Spanish version of the television program "This is Your Life" which devoted a show to Delibes in 1963, affirmed with some slight exaggeration: "After four years of marriage, he had four children and had written four novels." (The fourth novel in question could be a novelette, either "El loco" ["The Madman"] or "Los ráiles" ["The Rails"], both of which appeared separately in the lowcost "Novela del Sábado" series. Actually, the fourth long novel was published in 1953). Then, the script continued, "five years passed without children, and three without a novel, before the appearance of . . . *Sisí.*" The program concluded, "Discarding the idea which joins a bohemian life inseparably to literary creation, you live in peaceful and orderly fashion, as did your parents, and as you desire for your children. Teaching in the mornings, newspaper in the afternoons and evenings, novel during vacations, and hunting on Sundays . . .you dwell in the heart of Old Castile, with the internal peace of an old-time Christian, imprinting your life with all the parsimony of an ancient rite."

Such, indeed, was the tone of Delibes' life during many years, not monotonous, but characterized by steady, multiple activity, and punctuated only by the births of more children, further literary successes, and occasional travel. In 1954 appeared *La partida (The Departure)*, a collection of short stories, wherein the first and title story relates a young sailor's first day at sea, a tale which some critics believe to contain autobiographical content. One of the novelist's greatest successes was published in March of 1955, *Diario de un cazador (Diary of a Hunter)*, which was awarded the Miguel de Cervantes National Literary Prize. The same month, his departure coinciding with the novel's publication, Delibes made his first voyage to America, invited by the Circle of Journalists in Santiago, Chile, where during three months he lectured and subsequently toured parts of Brazil, Uruguay, and Argentina. These attainments were tempered by sadness, however, at the death of his father in August of the year at the age of eighty-one.

Delibes' travel experience was reflected in *Un novelista descubre América (A Novelist Discovers America)*, 1956, subsequently amplified with the incorporation of impressions of the Canary Islands and entitled *Por esos mundos (Round About the World)*. A further result is the emigration to Chile of Lorenzo, protagonist of *Diary of a Hunter*, in the sequel, *Diario de un emigrante (An Emigrant's Diary)*, 1958. Delibes relates that he received his first copy of the printed *Diary of a Hunter* in the airport en route to Chile, and explains in the foreword to the edition of these two novels in his *Complete Works* that, having read it on the plane and once more immersed himself in the character, it was more or less inevitable that his initial impressions were conditioned by the mentality of Lorenzo. Thus the second "Diary" has a definite autobiographical input. Both books share, in addition to the same protagonist and the passion for hunting, a fascinated interest in the popular speech of two areas, displaying the novelist's gifted transcription of the jargon of the man in the streets of two widely separate regions.

Meanwhile, a collected edition of four novelettes (some published previously as separate works) appeared with the title *Siestas con viento Sur (Siestas with the Southern Breeze)*, 1957, an alleged reference to one aspect of their composition: these works were drafted for the most part during the siesta hour of Delibes' summer vacations, and thus mentally linked with the south wind. This volume was awarded the Fastenrath Prize of the Royal Spanish Academy, and shortly afterward Delibes was invited to visit Italy, lecturing with favorable receptions in Milan, Turin, and Rome. This marked his first contact with foreign groups of professional Hispanists, and he was deeply moved by his discovery of the interest among non-Spanish-speaking people in Spain's literature and culture. Later the same year, he visited Portugal, lecturing in Coimbra and Lisbon, and became acquainted with the prominent Portuguese novelist, Fernando Namora.

During these years, Delibes also continued his newspaper career with considerable distinction. From 1952 until 1958, he was subdirector of *El norte de Castilla,* a period during which he was nominated repeatedly as director, but his name was rejected by the Ministry of Information, which had the power of veto in like situations throughout Spain. He was finally accepted for the directorship in 1958, and immediately began to give a more aggressive orientation to the newspaper, within a generally Christian Socialist ideology. He undertook a vigorous campaign for agrarian reforms and help to the Castilian peasant, ruined by years of drought and forgotten by the Government, which preferred to dedicate its aid programs to areas where the effect would be more immediate and evident. At the same time, he fought for a program of free and obligatory education which would coordinate the three existing levels (primary, secondary, and higher). He hired restless young writers willing to face the risks of writing in the controlled press of the day, and under his direction the paper's Sunday supplement "El caballo de Troya," "The Trojan Horse," published the most daring articles to appear in the Spanish press since the Civil War. His violent, determined campaign brought Delibes almost immediately under fire from Madrid, but he continued to resist the pressure (which included visits from the Ministers of Agriculture and Information, and a subsequent summons to Madrid) until May of 1963, when measures were taken forcing him to resign the directorship. Delibes capitulated, not because of threats toward himself, but because of imminent reprisals against his friends employed with *El Norte . . .* , whom the Government decided to hold responsible for any further offenses he might commit. Delibes subsequently explained that facing jail oneself is not the same morally as sending an innocent person instead. He has continued his association with the newspaper in a more passive role as member of its Board of Directors, his occasional collaborations less provocative in nature. It is ironic that these events took place shortly after the public proclamation of freedom of the press in Spain.

Social preoccupations are also reflected in the novels published during his years as director of *El norte . . . : La hoja roja (The Red Leaf)*, 1959, and *Las ratas (The Rats)*, 1962, the latter novel clearly related to the same issues that stimulated his campaign for agrarian and educational reforms. *The Rats* was awarded the Critics' Prize in the year following its publication, a recognition carrying the maximum literary prestige, in part because it is unendowed and no publisher profits from it; it represents the consensus of the nation's critics as to the best novel of the year. *The Red Leaf* was written with aid from the March Foundation, one of whose activities is the provision of funds to further the completion of works in progress judged to be of potential significance. The attainment of this award and of the Critics' Prize, in addition to prizes previously won, amounted to an official recognition of Delibes' stature as a novelist, now in possession of the most important awards for the novel existing in Spain. Obtaining the Critics' Prize was especially significant, following so close upon the unpleasant episodes with the Ministry of Information, as it signified something of a tacit endorsement by Spanish critics of Delibes' position.

At about the time he completed *The Rats*, Delibes stated in an interview: "My preoccupation with language goes no further than knowing the names of things and telling the story I have proposed in the fewest possible words."[18] While this may seem a simple and economical principle, "knowing the names of things" in the setting of which he writes is not easy. The peasant dialects in the isolated Castilian villages at times approach separate languages, incomprehensible not only for the Spaniard from another region or the man from the city, but sometimes unfamiliar even to the inhabitants of the next village. These local dialects are especially rich in names for the typical regional phenomena, but so localized that many terms used within some twenty miles of Valladolid were unknown, for example, to the novelist's wife, a lifelong resident of the area. This complicates diffusion of Delibes' works, particularly those dealing with rural Castile.

Despite the considerable linguistic or dialectic difficulties, some of Delibes' works have been translated (primarily to French, German, English, Italian, and Portuguese), and beginning approximately in 1958, he began to visit France more or less periodically, his journeys coinciding with the publication of translations of his narratives. In 1959 he traveled in Germany, finding himself already well known due to the translation of six of his books. This same year, he was able to fulfill a dream of many years with the construction of a cabin-refuge in a rural area near the Castilian village of Sedano, in the province of Burgos, a weekend and vacation retreat from civilization. In this isolated, wooded area, still uninvaded by radio, telephones, and television, Delibes built his "observatory of Castile," used as a headquarters for hunting and fishing expeditions, and ever-widening explorations of the surrounding countryside and villages. The contemporary-style cabin was not of flexible construction; when the younger children arrived and it was impossible to add more bunks, a hut was built nearby for the older boys. A direct result of observations in this area is *The Rats*, set in a nearby village, and the novelist's increasingly intimate knowledge of the plains of Castile is reflected in *La caza de la perdiz roja (Hunting the Red Partridge)*, 1963, *El libro de la caza menor (Small Game Hunting)*, 1964, *Viejas historias de Castilla la Vieja (Old Tales of Old Castile)* and

Castilla (Castile), likewise published in 1964. The last two titles contain the same text, but the latter is a deluxe edition for bibliophiles, a printing of 150 copies, with engravings by Jaume Plá.

Europa, parada y fonda (Europe, Stops and Inns), published in 1963, is a collection of travel impressions, mainly of Portugal, France, and Italy. Delibes and his wife undertook a trip to the United States in the autumn of 1964, where he spent a semester as Visiting Professor at the University of Maryland. The journey was marred by an unfortunate accident shortly before their departure, in which the two youngest of his seven children were seriously burned by boiling oil. Having accepted the commitment almost a year earlier, Delibes reluctantly left them in the care of his brother's family, but since then, despite many tempting offers, has refused to make any long-range contracts or to accept anything more than relatively brief lecture tours. Delibes' life in Maryland, and visits to various American universities in 1965, produced another travel book, *USA y yo (USA and I),* in 1966.

December of that year saw the publication of *Cinco horas con Mario (Five Hours with Mario),* a novel superficially quite different from Delibes' immediately preceding works, and surprising to those who had come to consider him first and foremost the novelist of Castilian towns and villages, of neorealistic technique and irony, light caricature and humor. These elements are submerged in *Five Hours with Mario,* in which interest centers upon character portrayal, the psychological analysis of the female protagonist, and the retrospective revelation of Mario's personality and their marital relationship. Nevertheless, the novel is less of a surprise in the context of Delibes' total work; although different in technique, it shares with his first two novels the protracted introspection, and with *The Path* its almost classical compression (both take place in a few hours in the mind of one central character). Despite the fact that Delibes himself while working on the novel considered it to be quite different from what he had done before,[19] when viewed in the perspective of his overall novelistic development, *Five Hours with Mario* has several specific antecedents. Its differences are primarily of narrative technique and emphasis, as many prior themes and settings reappear.

Vivir al día (Living from Day to Day), published in March of 1968, is not actually a new work; as the author explains in the prologue, it is a selection of his newspaper articles published over a period of some fifteen years, from 1953 to 1967. It does not include all reports and articles written during that time, but approximately one-third of them, and no attempt has been made to organize them thematically or otherwise. Following a strict chronological order, the book offers an interesting supplement to Delibes' mental history, elucidating extra-novelistic preoccupations, and may also throw additional light on the novels of the corresponding years. Beginning in an era when he had already authored four or five narrative volumes, these are articles written without literary or stylistic concern, or at least with less such intent than in pages destined from the outset to appear in book form. At times, Delibes' purpose may be much clearer, expressed in a simpler and more straightforward manner, because the articles were intended for a broader and less cultured public. They vary from the humorous sally to literary and theatrical criticism, to social reform and the metaphysical. Due to this variety, and their brevity and chronological exactness, these short essays are potentially more revealing of Delibes' concern at a given moment than the less numerous, more extensive works, manifesting his "psychological ups and downs, as well as those—no less extreme—of press censorship."[20] The title is explained in the prologue which refers to the economic difficulties of surviving as a writer in Spain, mentioning the fact that there the most profitable among generally unprofitable literary pursuits is the newspaper article, for which reason "the writer in Spain lives from day to day, or he does not live."

Shortly after publishing this collection, in the spring of 1968, Delibes spent a few weeks as the guest of universities in Czechoslovakia, leaving (in his words) "a society with which I was far from happy, to enter one I liked even less."[21] Despite this initially negative predisposition, he thrilled upon encountering the short-lived experiment in liberty and democracy within the Communist system, and while he had clear presentiments of the threat of the Russian invasion, he was sufficiently moved by this first visit to a Socialist country to write his testimonial volume, *La primavera de Praga (Springtime in Prague),* upon his return. The book was in press in August when the Russian invasion came, and Delibes had time only to add a brief foreword expressing his consternation and sorrow, mixed with hope that the light of liberty would not be extinguished completely. Dedicating the volume as a homage to the heroic people of Czechoslovakia and all others in history whose voices were stilled by force, he affirmed: "Arms may kill men, but they have never been able to kill ideas."[22] The book itself is an interesting revelation of Delibes' political thought, and it is implicit throughout that much of what he says applies in his own mind to

Spain, even though it is offered as a reminiscence about Czechoslovakia. Subsequently, the same publisher has printed a story collection entitled *La Mortaja (The Shroud)*, the tale giving the title having appeared previously in *Siestas with the Southern Breeze.* Also recently, as a collection for use in Spanish schools, Editorial Minon of Valladolid has published an anthology of Delibes' works, selecting chapters particularly appropriate for children. The title is *Mi mundo y el mundo (My World and the World).*[23] It contains fragments of various novels and travel books.

Parábola del naúfrago (Parable of the Drowning Man), published in the summer of 1969, is Delibes' latest novel to date. Like *Five Hours with Mario,* the book surprised many of his critics, who saw in it a complete break with the previous writings, a rejection of neo-realism in favor of extreme subjectivism, an attempt to imitate what appears to be the latest literary fad in Spain. Actually, as in the case of the novel immediately preceding, the break is more apparent than real. Many of Delibes' enduring themes are present, and the book as a whole turns upon one of the constants in his writing, the threat to the individual posed by the mechanized society. Although at times exacerbated and tending to the scatological, Delibes' characteristic humor is also present, and various incidents are anticipated in earlier works, specifically *Still It Is Day* and *My Adored Son Sisí*, but there are also antecedents in works such as *The Path* and *The Rats.* To what extent the new elements may be related to the visit to Czechoslovakia, shortly before writing this novel, or in the early days of its composition, is at present an imponderable. It seems inevitable that Delibes could not have had more than the slightest contact with intellectual and literary groups in Prague without hearing of Kafka, whose influence upon *Parable...* is suggested by one critic,[24] and he may have been stimulated either by the pending visit or afterwards to read that author's works. On the other hand, much of the floating anxiety and vague fears of the protagonist of *Parable...* can be discerned in various forms in Delibes' earlier works.

The mature Delibes (the Delibes of approximately the past five years) has not changed greatly in personality and habits from the young author of *Long Is the Cypress' Shadow,* although he has become more liberal with the years and progressively more disillusioned with reigning conditions in Spain. He admits to suffering great psychological oscillations, disproportionate to his circumstances, without cause or for insufficient reason. Of mercurial temperament, sad and high-spirited by turns, he qualifies himself as an asthenic, noting that mornings tend to stimulate and evenings to depress him. Whether exalted or depressed, however, "my opinion of the world is not too optimistic . . .its frivolity and violence . . ." Probably influenced by the philosophy of Ortega, and particularly by *The Revolt of the Masses* which he has read, he is preoccupied by the impression that the concerned minority is each day proportionately less. He fears and dislikes mass culture and psychology, refusing to have television because of what he considers its leveling influence: Delibes does not want his children to become conformists, with the same tastes as everyone else, although aware that in any case they go to other houses to watch the censured programs and pick up the tastes of their classmates. These influences he attempts to counterbalance with the effects of nature, with frequent isolation in the cabin in Sedano, and stimulating individuality wherever possible. He continues to feel his long-standing aversion to mechanization, and commented that once a town acquires traffic lights, he begins to dislike it.

The novelist and his numerous family occupy a large apartment in a relatively new building in one of the nicer sections of Valladolid, their home furnished comfortably and with good taste in a fashion between Spanish and international-contemporary, although without luxuries. He and his wife particularly enjoy books on art, but have a large collection of other recent books, especially novels. Another hobby is colored slides. Despite his travels, Delibes continues to prefer Spanish, and more particularly Castilian, cooking. His own culinary specialty is *paella*, which he makes over an open fire in the wilderness. During the four months the hunting season lasts, he goes hunting every Sunday; then trout season opens; and he attempts to fish at least one day a week. He is also an avid swimmer, and has transmitted most of his avocations to his children.

As a Catholic, Delibes was very favorably impressed by the reforms of Pope John XXIII, having felt at times too restricted within the Spanish Church's dogmatic interpretations, which he compared to a straitjacket. While considering himself to be an orthodox believer, he is interested in implementing liberal changes within the church in Spain, particularly the Vatican II conciliar acts and the ecumenical movement. He also wishes to give a more social character to the activities of the Spanish Church, and would like to see it increasingly active in the eradication of poverty and social injustice.

Another preoccupation of Delibes, not preponderant in his writing, but nonetheless of long standing, is pacifism. This is directly traceable to his experiences in the Spanish Civil War, but has been reinforced during years of living in a world in constant tension, and perhaps given special and renewed impetus by the armed suppression of Czechoslovakia's experiment in freedom, so keenly felt by the novelist. While some expression of this antiwar attitude is found in his first novel and in various articles and sections of the travel books, it has heretofore been in his life rather than in literature that Delibes has most evinced his pacifistic convictions. However, at present he is at work on an antiwar novel whose proposed title is "Las guerras de mis antepasados" ("The Wars of My Forefathers").[25]

Delibes' wife continues to be extremely important in his life, as a stabilizing psychological influence and as his secretary and "first reader." A keen observer whom he terms a "sage critic," she is also helpful in calling his attention to many details of the sort which a woman is more likely to notice, such as changes in the cloth traditionally used by the peasants for their clothing. While it would be inexact to describe her as coauthor, the importance of her collaboration is considerable. According to the novelist, she is also a constant stimulus for his work. He writes by hand, and always in the same spot, with an almost indecipherable although attractive caligraphy.

The outstanding personality trait of Delibes would seem to be consistency, firmness of character, and a certain uniformity or persistence, as shown first by his fidelity to his father's example, his independent intellectual solitude in Valladolid, and the long-lasting nature of his basic beliefs and habits. With the passing years, he has progressed from the conservatism of the family in which he was raised toward a Christian Socialism and greater liberalism within the bounds of Catholicism, but in both religion and politics he is undogmatic, sincerely respecting the rights of others. The fundamental patterns of his life and work, however, are essentially those established in childhood and adolescence: the same hobbies, the same passion for nature, and the same energetic, multiple channeling of activity. His travels have given him a new awareness of Spain and Castile, an ever greater interest in the peculiar character of life and language in the surrounding villages and countryside, a progressively more intense interest in others. These are not radical changes, however; this is evolution within a perceptible basic pattern. Much the same will be seen in the following study of his works, where artistic progress is not equivalent to a break with the past, but to a steady development.

A letter from Delibes dated October 28, 1970, mentions that the literary periodical, *Destino*, of Barcelona, began a series of articles (apparently a type of memoirs) which the novelist calls his "impressions," the first appearing in the issue of Sunday, October 25, 1970. Completion of the present study cannot be postponed indefinitely in order to include the series, but presumably this will be useful to future investigators both in terms of more ample biographical and personal data, and further revelations of the personality and opinions of one of contemporary Spain's leading literary figures.

CHAPTER 2

The First Two Novels

LA SOMBRA del ciprés es alargada (Long Is the Cypress' Shadow) and Aún es de día (Still It Is Day) may be treated together not only because of their proximity in time (the first was published in 1948 and the second in 1949), but also because of many stylistic similarities. Rhetorically, both are ponderous and at times ornate, with long sentences, much introspection, and lengthy paragraphs with limited dialogue in comparison with most later works. However, they belong together for other reasons, including the fact that many critics link them, some as opposites, others as the product of the novelist's "first phase." They are opposites in terms of the dominant psychology of the respective protagonists: Pedro, in the former, is characterized by enduring pessism, and Sebastián, in the latter, often exemplifies an optimism quite out of keeping with his circumstances. Inasmuch as the second novel probably represents Delibes' reaction to criticism of the first, an attempt to remedy what were seen as faults of the earlier work, they are also closely related in conception. Then, too, both novels share a common religious solution to, or sublimation of, problems raised therein, and are largely philosophical and moralistic, even if one agrees that the philosophies are in some respects opposed. This basic polarity is reflected by the imagery of the titles, one emphasizing darkness and the other, light.

In the prologue to the first volume of his *Obra Completa (Complete Works)*,[1] Delibes confesses his lack of literary formation when composing the early novels, remarking that his reading in those years was "at the dictate of the critics. When *The Cypress* . . . was compared to Proust, I began to read Proust; when Galdós was mentioned in connection with *Still It Is Day*, I sought Galdós. But the truth is that I wrote my first three novels as much by instinct as would have been the case had I decided to build a ship." Hostile critics blamed Delibes for a supposedly anti-intellectual attitude because of this affirmation, and an implicit vaingloriousness in his denial of prior influences,[2] but facts do not support this interpretation. Rather, Delibes was speaking in all humility, as indicated by his willingness to learn from the critics and to change his works accordingly. Despite the skeptical irony which met the statement quoted above, there seems to be little basis to qualify as anti-intellectual a writer who holds the equivalent of the doctorate in two areas, and has done advanced study in a third. In an interview in 1963, when asked his judgment of this first novel, Delibes stated that he considered it mediocre, bad, not for what it lacked but for the things it has in excess, petulance and ingenuousness.[3] However, he would not renounce or destroy this first attempt, even were it feasible, for "no one has the right to deny his first steps."

The novelist's preface cited above indicates that he links the first novels in his own mind, together with the third, as works written "instinctively," without consciousness of specific literary principles or aims. At the same time, these narratives belong to the period when Delibes was most receptive to criticism, and many differences in the first three works may result from negative critiques of the first two novels. While more recent criticism, with hindsight, has considered the first two novels "frustrated attempts," it should not be forgotten that upon appearance they met with favorable and even enthusiastic reception.

I Long Is the Cypress' Shadow

Delibes' first novel, like many novelists' first efforts, has a considerable autobiographic content, although it is definitely not an autobiography. The protagonist resembles his creator in the pre-occupation with death, fear of losing those he loves, and in his pessimism. However, while Delibes' pessimism is not the result of conditioning events in his childhood, there are many determining factors in the protagonist's (Pedro's) youth which combine to convince him of the rightness of a pessimistic outlook and the necessity of his philosophy of nonengagement, or noninvolvement with others, in order to minimize personal suffering. And, as the novelist noted later, he pushed the obsession to the extreme in this work, allowing it to inhibit most of Pedro's life, while it was not permitted to reach a similar extreme in his own life. Pedro, like his creator, is religious (at least in theory), and certain other specifics are shared, such as the interest in a naval career, which becomes reality in Pedro's life, while renounced by Delibes. The concrete situations, however, are mostly quite different.

Pedro from childhood is bereft of all that Delibes enjoyed in family and domestic life, and denied even the comfort of friendship by his young companion's untimely death.

One commentator has asserted that Enrique Larreta's novel, *La gloria de Don Ramiro,* influenced the conception of *The Cypress . . . ,* inasmuch as both protagonists have severe upbringing in Avila, one that predetermines a pessimistic outlook and inclines them to flee the world's temptations, although both eventually succumb.[4] However, these similarities are quite superficial, and seem rather to be accidental coincidences than influences. In Larreta's novel, there was a specific aesthetic intent to write in the style of *modernismo,*[5] definitely absent in Delibes, and the latter has very little of the spatial and temporal exoticism of the former. True, Delibes' first novel has a relative "exoticism," compared with the narrowly local settings of later works. Rather than being limited to Valladolid, the early chapters take place in the not-too-distant Castilian city of Avila, and toward the end there is an excursion (probably an artistic error) into territory unknown to the novelist, our New England area. However, Delibes does not concentrate on exotic aspects of either locale, nor are they introduced with that purpose. In technique, style, "message," and emphasis, Larreta's novel and Delibes' are very different, and even the plots diverge widely after the vaguely similar points of departure.

Most articles written after the publication of *The Cypress . . .* were polemic, tending to question the decision of the Nadal judges who awarded the prize to Delibes, or to defend them and the novelist himself against attacks by supporters of the other major contender, Pombo Angulo. With few exceptions, this criticism does little to illumine or explain the novel. Critiques written afterward, when the heat of the polemic had died, dismissed the first novels as inferior to later works, so little has been written on Delibes' novels preceding *The Path* which evaluates or explores them in and for themselves.

Those few reviews or studies which gave attention to more strictly literary matters mentioned similarities with Proust, insofar as *The Cypress . . .* is also a novel in *tempo lento,* introspective and retrospective, with exterior action almost nonexistent, while providing minute description of interior action or psychological events. One critic suggested that Delibes' most immediate antecedent among Spanish novelists was Pío Baroja (an observation yet more justifiable after the appearance of *Still It Is Day),* and another compared Delibes' portrait of the moribund provincial atmosphere with the manner of Dickens.

Some basis exists for these comparisons, but readers familiar with the considerable differences between the writers cited will realize that at times the foundations must be rather slight. If Delibes had a model upon writing *The Cypress* . . .(and he has said that consciously he had none), the most likely candidate is Baroja. Even with the small literary background he acknowledges during his early days as a writer, it is quite unlikely that Delibes would have been totally unfamiliar with the works of the leading living Spanish novelist.

The example of Baroja need not have been a conscious influence, but there are definite similarities with his *El árbol de la ciencia,* specifically in the central symbolism of both novels, employing in each case two trees as symbols of life and death. These trees become obsessions of the respective protagonists, both of whom are paralyzed by introspection and suffering from abulia, a weakness of will. Both have developed a philosophy of voluntary self-detachment from life as a shield from the pain of loss and disappointments. Neither really believes in the possibility of true happiness, and both desert their philosophical positions to marry, with tragic results. The structure of both works is rather loose, autobiographical, anecdotal and discursive, and each contains long conversations on ethics, which help to confirm the protagonist in the detached stance toward which previous experiences have already inclined him. The outcome differs, no doubt largely because of Delibes' orthodox Catholicism. Where Baroja's protagonist chose suicide after the death of his wife and unborn child, Pedro rejects this alternative in similar circumstances, in favor of a not-too-felicitous religious solution. Whether or not the example of Baroja was a conscious influence (and it has been so well assimilated that probably it was not), the coincidences seem more numerous than should happen by mere chance. There is no doubt, though, that *The Cypress* . . . is an original and independent work, by no means a simple imitation.

Delibes' earliest novel is divided into two parts, the first superior to the second in the opinion of most critics. This may be due to hasty writing of the second part in order to finish for the Nadal judging, or to the fact that most of this part deals with things less familiar to the author than is the case with the preceding division. Part I relates the life of Pedro in Avila, in the home of his tutor, Don Mateo Lesmes, with whom he went to live at the age of ten. The boy's parents are dead and he has little recollection of them or of his life up to the time when he was left with Don Mateo by his uncle. He receives a bare minimum of warmth from his tutor's family, and Don Mateo himself is cold, stoic, and pessimistic, accepting only from economic necessity the burden of Pedro and a second child, Alfredo, whose mother has left him there because he interferes with her love affair. Don Mateo inculcates in young Pedro his philosophy of noninvolvement, teaching that in order not to be unhappy, one must renounce all emotional ties to life, every relationship with the world, including love, friendship, and family, since all human involvement implies pain and loss. Only a complete break guarantees a painless life, serenity, indifference, and neutrality. The death of Alfredo, with whom Pedro had become emotionally involved despite his teacher's warning, seemed to prove the wisdom of Don Mateo's philosophy, and in his bereavement and suffering the boy determined henceforth to flee life and love so as to avoid future wounds. Largely for this reason, and in the absence of any real vocation, he chose a career in the merchant marine, as endless travel would minimize the possibility of his maintaining any relationship long enough to become vulnerable.

The cypress of the novel's title is a tree found primarily in cemeteries in Spain, so it automatically evokes funereal associations, and in the novel its shadow represents both the eternal darkness, and the obsession of death for the protagonist. He visits a cemetery on two occasions in the first part, upon the death of a young classmate, and for the burial of Alfredo. Alfredo felt a particular horror of the cypress, and asked to be buried beneath a pine, which thereby acquires a life symbolism. For the purposes of the book, the pine's shadow is considered to be spherical, round, and emblematic of plenitude, while the shadow of the cypress is elongated, needlelike, and inseparably linked with pessimism, melancholy, withdrawal, and nothingness. A parallel symbolism attributes similar qualities to the shadows of men: those of optimists are round, and those of pessimists, like that of the cypress.

The second part is preceded by a quotation from the Book of Genesis, "It is not good that man should live alone," but living alone is what Pedro does for most of the novel, from the death of Alfredo, through five years more with Don Mateo, then in the Naval School in Barcelona, and finally at sea. A ship within a bottle becomes a symbol of his "protected" existence, from which he perceives the world as through a glass, but without really coming into contact with it. Some years later, while still young but approaching middle age, he meets an Irish-American girl, Jane, with whom he falls in love despite himself, and deserting his creed of nonengagement, marries her. Briefly they are happy; then he undertakes a final voyage alone, to return to Spain and prepare a home. He learns that his wife is expecting a child, and for the first time allows himself thoughts of a family, the future, and domesticity. However, as his ship arrives back in Providence, his wife, who has come to meet him, dies before his eyes as her car is forced from the dock into the waters of the port. The abrupt loss of family and future stuns him; time becomes meaningless. He resumes his existence on the former basis, believing that it was a mistake to have forsaken his philosophy, but treasuring his grief and loneliness, which become his reason for living.

Perhaps the novel should have ended here; it might have been less satisfactory for the author, but would have carried more psychological conviction. In the final pages, however, Pedro experiences a sudden and rather poorly motivated but overwhelming desire to return to Avila, which he finds covered with snow, as was Jane's body when last he saw her. He begins to identify her with Avila, and afterward, en route to the cemetery, links her with Alfredo, whose tomb he visits and into which he casts her wedding ring, an act from which he derives a mystic comfort. Then, although he has not remembered them in years, he leaves the cemetery thinking fondly of his tutor and Don Mateo's family, which fills him with surprising plenitude. "And besides, there was God," the closing words, are likewise somewhat unconvincing, as this religious sublimation or "conversion" is somehow more of a surprise for the reader than Pedro's renunciation of his solitude which had apparently become too much of a burden to be borne alone. While the intervening motivation is insufficient, it would seem that the novelist did not mean the final change of attitude to be a complete surprise, for in a sense Pedro completes a cycle or circle as he comes back to the cemetery and Alfredo's grave, where he first embraced the philosophy of noninvolvement, to reject it. Psychologically, Pedro has somehow returned to the moment of Alfredo's death, which he originally rebelled against, finally accepting it as God's will, and the pending reunion with the tutor's family also symbolizes a return to the beginnings.

Hickey[6] suggests that Delibes' purpose in presenting this character was to illustrate the gap—frequent in Spanish Catholicism—between faith and works, or between religion and life. Pedro is seen as typifying those who have no problem in believing, in a passive sense, but whose belief is not translated into action. Thus, his faith does not serve him for living, except in a very negative dimension (not committing suicide);

it adds no joy to his life and brings him no closer to his fellowman. Hickey notes the tremendous dichotomy between Pedro's lip service to religion and his way of life, and alleges that Delibes conceived the character as an object lesson in the necessity of intergrating faith and works.

While some critics wished to see *The Cypress* . . . as a thesis novel supporting Pedro's stance, Delibes was far from advocating this policy of noninvolvement, despite the convincing exposition of his protagonist's initial adoption thereof. Even though the novel's close is insufficiently motivated, it is evident that the author intended that Pedro should ultimately realize that his philosophy was in effect a death-in-life, as is clear when he returns to Alfredo's tomb and embraces the pine, symbolizing life, with their two names carved upon it, and then goes forth from the cemetery like one risen from the dead. The citation from the Book of Genesis makes this even more obvious, and any further doubt can be dispelled by comparison with the example of Delibes' own life. While aspects of his psychological makeup at least potentially resembled Pedro's, he chose the opposite of non-involvement, and with his other consistencies of personality, it is inconceivable that he should devote an entire novel to arguing against that vital decision.

II Still It Is Day

The similarities and points of contact between Delibes' first two novels, discussed at the beginning of this chapter, might be enlarged upon, but while numerous, they do not outweigh the differences. This can be deduced prior to comparing the novels from the fact that none of the articles written subsequent to the publication of *Still It Is Day* mentioned the writers previously invoked, such as Proust and Dickens, while various critics began to speak of Naturalism or to debate whether the second novel was naturalistic or realistic. The novelist subsequently declared that his intent was realism, that he lacked sufficient knowledge of Naturalism at that stage to have attempted it. Then, too, parts of naturalistic ideology such as materialism and determinism would have been automatically unacceptable to him, yet some critics opined that Delibes' criteria were "excessively deterministic."[7] It is true that in the first novel the influence of early surroundings and education is decisive for many years, yet, however unconvincingly the conclusion is handled, it is obviously the novelist's intent that at last that influence be shaken off. And in *Still It Is Day,* the protagonist attempts from the beginning to better himself through the exercise of something clearly similar to free will. That he is unable to change fully the character of others (even while making some progress in that direction), and that his socio-economic milieu is likewise beyond the efforts of one person to change, may justify in some measure those who find pessimism in Delibes' second novel as well, but this is much more realistic than the pessimism of Pedro, based as it is on external rather than on subjective factors. And the attribution of determinism is hardly exact, for Sebastián does not sink into the spiritual and physical mire which surround him, but concentrates his psychic energy upon rising above his circumstances. Even if he succeeds only in extracting himself spiritually, the novel is less than deterministic.

The protagonist, Sebastián, a poor, deformed, and dwarfish hunchback in his early twenties, is the incarnation of almost incurable optimism. He lives in sordid surroundings, with an alcoholic mother (the vulgar former servant of his deceased father), and thirteen-year-old Orencia, his mother's daughter, born eleven months after his father's death. The mother, Aurelia, insists that Orencia is the daughter of her deceased husband, and Sebastián unquestioningly considers her his sister. Their relationship is close, as each attempts to find in the other some escape from solitude and loneliness, and from Aurelia's harsh indifference. The psychology of Sebastián is fairly well delineated on the first page: "For twenty years, he had thought each morning upon waking that the day could bring a radical change in his existence. It never occurred to him to imagine what that change might be. He was satisfied with the wish, the vague hope that it might be some renewal, something that would break the sad monotony of his regular, gray life."[8] Throughout the novel, Sebastián continues to hope, desire, and expect, despite frustrations, setbacks, emotional and economic tragedies, and other events which should have been profoundly disillusioning. A marriage is arranged for him by his mother, as Aurora, the ugly daughter of a rather wealthy black marketeer, is pregnant and needs a husband. When faced with betrayal, the discovery of the falseness of his mother and fiancée, he retreats into religion, and while at the conclusion he accepts a measure of reality, he does so with spiritual armor between himself and his surroundings.

The action begins in 1946, so that the novel portrays aspects of the Spanish economy and social structure in the year or two preceding its composition, and by implication indicts their injustice (an aspect which has escaped most commentators). That such was Delibes' intent is clear from his inclusion of *Still It Is Day* in the third volume of his *Complete Works,*[9] together with the two other novels which voice his strongest social criticism up to that point, *The Red Leaf* and *The Rats.* In the prologue to the volume just mentioned, the novelist states that the common denominator of the three novels is the "sentiment of the Other," which "some call social unrest or social preoccupation, an adjective—social—which, if it were not so worn with use, so limited to a single aspect of human relatedness, I would have gladly adopted."[10] He then explains his rejection, noting that the type of writing presently designated by the term "social novel" is too simplistic in focus, reducing all humanity to rich and poor, capitalists and workers, with the wealthy being aggressive, heartless exploiters, and the poor patient, submissive, and exploited. In other words, the rich are by definition evil, and those who are not rich, are good. Thus, in order for virtue to triumph, there must be revolution. Within this statement of the problem, a novelist is limited to portraying the *dolce vita* of the rich, their hypocrisy and lack of sensitivity, or else to exposing the wounds, humiliation, and suffering of the lower classes, unless he contrives some combination of the two. While Delibes is completely in agreement that social reforms are urgently needed in Spain, he does not accept this division of humanity, strictly on a class basis, into victims and executioners. Also, although he believes the need for a more equitable distribution of wealth is pressing, he does not think that this will solve all problems. Nor can he swallow the notion that the rich are necessarily bad and the poor inevitably good, any more than the contrary possibility. Not only is he too much of a realist, but his Christian ethics produce reservations. Then, too, as he sees it, this measure would not solve the dilemmas of human solitude and communication, and other civic and educational problems.

Still It Is Day was much more severely treated by the censor than its predecessor, with some twenty cuts, a few of them extensive. The intention can be assumed to have been to "clean up" the work, but at times the censor's intervention had the opposite effect, seeming to pull a veil across certain scenes and suggesting thereby even obscene interpretations. Therefore, before publishing the novel again in his *Complete Works,* Delibes requested the original manuscript from the censor's office, as it was the only extant copy of the complete version. He received an affirmative reply, but after several years of waiting in which the manuscript was not returned, he rewrote material for the censored passages and—since it was necessarily a revised version—pruned and polished a few other pages. Thus, this particular novel is not the same in the *Complete Works* as in editions prior to 1968, although the differences are seldom large.

Orencia is treated almost as a slave by her mother, who apparently hates both her children, although living on Sebastián's small wage. Aurelia delights in reminding her son of his deformity and the fact that he inherited it from his father, calling both "horrible, deformed puppets." She discourages Sebastián's thoughts of advancement, alleging that for better positions, a more decorative man is needed. While he suffers inwardly, he gives no outward sign. Except for Orencia's room, the house is a garbage heap of dirty newspapers, dead cockroaches, orange peels and peanut shells, rat manure, and empty bottles, evidence of Aurelia's frequent binges. The tenement in which they live is old, dirty, unheated, with its peeling vestibule decorated wtih obscene drawings and graffiti.

Sebastián's main ambition is to obtain a better job, not only to escape from the all-too-similar atmosphere of the neighborhood grocery and black market where he is employed, but to leave behind the area's repugnant moral atmosphere. When he succeeds, despite his physical defects, in being accepted as errand boy in a fashionable textile store, Sebastián considers himself a conquering hero, imagines that he is the envy of the neighborhood, and even fancies that his father, somewhere above, contemplates his triumph with satisfaction. This exaggerated evaluation of such limited success indicates, by implication, the difficulties of advancement in Spanish society (other than by dishonest methods, the black market, and so on), and reflects the severe economic straits of a majority of Spaniards at the time of the novel's composition.

Still It Is Day is set entirely in Valladolid, mostly in the center near the City Market, with one or two sallies into the surrounding countryside, as Sebastián escapes upon occasion to refresh himself in the open fields. Much attention is given to the description of this crumbling section of the city, and there is considerable analysis of the minor commercial employees of Almacenes Suárez, the store where Sebastián is employed during most of the novel. There are two more or less simultaneous lines of development, one connected with Sebastián's home life, and the other with his time in the store. Working zealously, he advances to the position of sales clerk, while attempting to bring some improvement in his home life. By contrivance of the two mothers, he has become engaged to Aurora, daughter of the prosperous black marketeer for whom he previously worked, Aurora, pregnant, has been abandoned by her boyfriend, and her mother pays Aurelia to arrange the match. At first, Sebastián attributes Aurora's sudden interest in him to his new position, but little Orencia informs him of the truth.

As a counterpoint to his relationship with the horribly plain and vulgar Aurora, Sebastián has another "love," which opens a world of fantasy to him. Irene, a beautiful, wealthy young client of Almacenes Suárez inspires an overwhelming infatuation, and he lives only for glimpses of her. Aware that he can never hope to attract her physically or socially, he comes to imagine that he will have a chance if only he can make her see the hidden beauty of his soul. He directs at her a barrage of his most "soulful" looks, but the lovely Irene is indifferent, either unaware, or aware sadistically, for upon one occasion she asks whether he has an eye defect, and comments that it seems he is trying to display before her innocent gaze all the obscenity of his soul. Impulsively, Sebastián keeps a glove she left forgotten on a counter, changing his original intention of returning it for the chance of having a relic of his beloved. However, a search is launched in the store, and eventually Sebastián resorts to a clumsy farce of "finding" the glove, which fools no one and results in his dismissal.

Meanwhile, he has melodramatically broken with Aurora, despite Aurelia's opposition, and has begun to frequent a church in another neighborhood, where he is influenced by the sermons and conversation of Padre Matías, a Capuchin friar.[11] He begins to have nightmares after the suicide of another pregnant girl in the neighborhood, nightmares which synthesize all his complex emotional preoccupations and reveal a sense of responsibility toward Aurora's unborn child. Although the dreams vary, each has the dead baby and some sort of punishment for Sebastián. He attempts to take refuge in more intense religiosity, in further "perfecting" of his soul, but concludes, despite his unwavering spiritual fidelity to Irene, that his duty is to marry Aurora and be a father to her child, particularly after the real progenitor is killed by Aurora's brother in a bar. This decision comes only hours before the loss of his job, and his first subsequent reaction is that he cannot marry Aurora now, because everyone will think that he is doing so for her father's money. However, he concludes that this will give his sacrifice more meaning, since no one will see it in its true light, and thus his virtue will not be vainglorious. He decides at the novel's end that they will marry and live as brother and sister, raising the child no one had wanted.

The entire action of the novel, exclusive of flashbacks and retrospective material, occupies some five months. While there is considerable external, and even extraneous action, the most important action is internal, the analysis of Sebastián's inferiority complex, his suffering at the cruel jokes of comrades, and the almost complete lack of others' understanding. Also very significant are his feelings of having been exploited emotionally, and deceived by his mother and Aurora. All of this leads or contributes to a religious experience of sorts, the climax of Sebastián's struggle. Hickey[12] chooses to call it a conversion, alleging that the novel as a whole is the history of a progression toward more perfect faith. This may, indeed, have been Delibes' intention. On the other hand, it is perfectly possible to interpret Sebastián's suddenly increased religiosity as a sublimation of his hopeless love for Irene. While the novelist probably did not intend it so, Sebastián's idealized passion is grotesque, although it is perfectly integrated into the other elements. In the final resolution, Sebastián seems to intend to continue to "purify" himself through lifelong suffering, possibly implying the sin of pride, although Hickey sees it as authentic asceticism. The protagonist does formulate a plan to impart to the completely unidealized Aurora something of the platonic exaltation he has experienced through his love for Irene, as he envisions a similarly ideal relationship when he decides: "We will live like brother and sister, raising that child which neither of us wanted."

Certainly, there are scenes in the novel which can be classified as naturalistic in their detailing of repugnant details and events, but Delibes' emphasis is on Sebastián's spiritual evolution, and this alone excludes deterministic intent. True, most of the action takes place in an environment that is physically and sometimes morally depressing, somber, and occasionally disgusting (for example, the scenes involving Aurora's senile grandmother). Nevertheless, Sebastián continues for the most part his optimistic outlook, despite a momentary crisis when, having broken with Aurora, he feels the passing attraction of suicide, not because he loved her enough to justify this, but because he is humiliated, disillusioned, and tired of struggling.

The situation at the close of the novel suggests that some progress is possible, that in Sebastián's situation one can make strides toward rehabilitating an alcoholic mother or bringing light into the sister's joyless life. In other words, he can give his own life the value he chooses to impart by the ethical principles he follows. The pessimism some observers have attributed to *Still It Is Day* is very relative: it consists in admitting that some people live in extremely difficult circumstances, not all of which can be voluntarily remedied, or which lie beyond the means of one person to change. At the same time, Delibes makes it quite clear that even under the worst conditions, one has a broad range of alternative attitudes among which to choose.

Hickey, whose orientation is primarily religious, notes in the study previously cited that, with the exception of Sebastián, characters in the first two novels (and most later works) are either lacking in charity, or neutral in that regard. In the two earliest novels, he observes, even that charity par excellence, maternal love, is absent. It may be excessively simplistic to see in these works only a religious thesis-by-omission, although the affirmation that Delibes' intention was to paint the consequences of lack of charity is supported in part by the novelist's statement that his second novel was the result of his preoccupation for "the Other." Certainly, the subjective aspects of religion and ethics loom larger in the first works. and while Delibes may not have intended to write what is known as a "Catholic novel," he was undoubtedly concerned to a large extent with Christian ethics.

The first two novels are now considered inferior to Delibes' later production, but by no means are they entirely bad. The reader may not accept the philosophies or solutions offered, but he will not be bored. These two novels served in their day to introduce a considerable narrative talent, and helped the novelist to perfect himself in his art. In *Still It Is Day,* Delibes takes a step in the direction of altruistic concerns, away from the intense subjectivism of *Long Is the Cypress' Shadow,* even though the technique continues to be subjective. The second novel is more concentrated in time and space, anticipating such later works as *The Path* and *Five Hours with Mario,* and also contains examples of Delibes' characteristic humor, absent in its solemn predecessor. In both, many constants of his work are present, particularly the concern for the individual in relation to society, the obsession with death, the curative power of nature, the problem of human solitude, and the interest in adolescent or juvenile figures. While one cannot obtain a complete picture of Delibes from the first two novels, neither can any reasonably thorough study overlook them or simply dismiss them as inferior to his later work.

CHAPTER 3

El camino (The Path)

DELIBES' third novel, *El camino (The Path)*, shows an intensification of the refining and simplifying process begun in *Still It Is Day*. It is much shorter, perhaps half the length of its predecessors, and while flashback material covers several years, the action as such takes place in one night, as the eleven-year-old protagonist and central consciousness, Daniel, sleeplessly awaits the morning when for the first time he will leave his native mountain village for school in the "city" (presumably a nearby provincial capital). During this last night at home, memories crowd his mind, and through his eyes the reader becomes acquainted with a gallery of picturesque characters, most if not all the village's inhabitants, with their histories, and major events in Daniel's life. Little more can be said of the plot or structure, for plan and action have been subordinated to interest in character presentation, and to the portrayal of a special environment. Upon this slender thread of plot are hung a large number of anecdotes, some verging on the tragic, others comic, some lyric, and others grotesque.

Certain observers have wished to see a thesis in *The Path*, taking as their point of departure a sermon by the parish priest, Don José ("who was a great saint"). Don José stated from the pulpit that everyone has a "path" in life, and that to depart from it was displeasing to God.[1] In Daniel's elementary understanding, his "path" was to remain in the village and one day to replace his father in the family cheese factory. Of course, underlying this was a typical youngster's reluctance to leave his family and friends in order to study, clearly presented on the opening page. The village school apparently offered the first grades only, and in order to obtain his *bachillerato* (roughly the equivalent of a high school diploma), the boy had to spend several years in the city; this to his father meant "progress." The same critics who believe that the thesis of *The Path* is that Daniel should remain in the village assume an ultraconservative, antieducational, antiprogressive bias on Delibes' part.

51

But the apparent simplicity of *The Path* (and various other works) may be deceptive. The "message" of the book is more complex than these interpretations indicate, for if Delibes had intended Don José's sermon to be the basis of a thesis, why should he treat him mockingly or ironically, as many of the same critics observe? The most accurate appraisal would be to say that the work is a product of Delibes' concern, underlying *The Red Leaf, The Rats,* and other writings, for the uprooted peasant or villager in the city. It is not so much that "the city is evil" as that there is a cultural gap of centuries between life there and in the countryside.

From the publication of *The Path* onward, it became commonplace to speak of the city-country dichotomy in Delibes' work, and to identify the city with "progress" and the country with relative virtue, peace of mind, and lack of change. An extreme example of this viewpoint attributes to Delibes a "pessimistic vision of contemporary civilization, of technology, of the city . . .an attitude, there is no doubt, typically reactionary."[2] This, however, is an oversimplification, quite unjustified considering Delibes' daring newspaper campaign in favor of free public education, of agricultural, social, and religious reforms. And even if Daniel is against "progress" when equated with going to the city, this does not mean that he speaks for the author. Had the novelist wished to present this seriously as a thesis, he surely could have chosen a more convincing spokesman than an inexperienced, unschooled eleven-year-old villager, who psychologically is still very much a child. Another observer, who stated that for Delibes "virtue is in the country and sin in the city,"[3] was not motivated by the hostility of the critic previously cited, but likewise has oversimplified. Both statements are based on several novels, not on *The Path* alone, but as Delibes' third work is one of his most successful and best-known, it is frequently invoked as proof when these and similar affirmations are made.

The novelist has elucidated these questions somewhat in the prologues to the first and second volumes of his *Complete Works.*[4] In the prologue to Volume One, which included *The Path*, he wrote: "I attribute the success of *The Path* to the fact that in this book we see ourselves when we were children, that it helps us to reconstruct a world—the world of · childhood—brutally annihilated by modern technology. . . .The nostalgia of that age in which human weaknesses are seen without bitterness, and daily contact with mediocrity and death has still not formed a layer of skepticism in us, is undoubtedly the fundamental reason . . ." Continuing, he expounded upon his preference for primitive or elementary characters (including children, adolescents, and the uneducated or mentally retarded), usually in rural settings: "For me, the novel is the man, and man, in his authentic, spontaneous reactions ... is only found, at the present level of civilization (?) in the villages." The fact that Delibes does not see today's mechanized civilization as an unmixed blessing does not make him a reactionary, nor does his understanding a small boy's reluctance to leave home mean that because he portrays dolts, drunkards, and fanatics, he is proposing them as models for imitation.

Besides explaining his preference for the more spontaneous rural personalities, Delibes offers another reason for his fondness for the country in the prologue to Volume Two: "... my propensity to what is rural and the instinctive tenderness with which I customarily wrap these areas and their inhabitants ... may signify, rather than recognition of the virtues of the country, a feeling of pity because of its abandonment. In other words, the countryside is full of vice, but its inhabitants are not responsible; on the other hand, urban vice is more self-conscious, a vice not forged, except on certain social levels, by sordidness and ignorance, but by tedium and refinement. Thus the sins of the country are not only more primitive than the urban ones, but more excusable." Regarding the notion that he sees virtue in the country and sin in the city, Delibes replied that if such were the case he would write only of the city, as vice offers more possibilities for the novelist than virtue. In several works, then, Delibes chooses to paint rural life and people because he finds them more spontaneous and prefers subjects without the veneer of civilization, people who are elementary rather than oversocialized and hypocritical in their reactions. Clearly, however, he does not idealize or admire them, but rather is moved, as he states, by pity, and hence the considerable impulse for social reform contained in these works.

It seems difficult to imagine, some twenty years later and outside Spain, how so innocuous a work as *The Path* could have provoked some of the reactions that followed its publication. For example, a program of the Spanish National Radio in Barcelona aired the opinion of a critic who quite mistakenly identified this novel as part of the movement called *tremendismo,* and applied to *The Path* such descriptive terms as "crude" and "festering."[5] Rather startling also is the verdict in a newspaper article that the novel contained "many censurable ... crudities," including crude language, an outspokenness "bordering on irreverence," and that the novel should be read "only by persons with adequate moral preparation."[6] Such evaluations are of course relative, and say more about the political climate in which they were produced than the work in question. As a counterbalance, there were other opinions, such as that of Antonio Vilanova in *Destino*, that *The Path* was "the most perfect masterpiece of the (Spanish) contemporary novel, which in its apparent lack of transcendence, possesses eternal values . . ." The favorable, laudatory, and even superlative far outnumbered the negative commentaries. Present opinion in Spain is totally favorable, and a movie based on the novel was produced in 1965 by Ana Mariscal.

Subsequent to publication of *The Path,* it became common to consider Delibes a novelist of adolescence, based largely on the youthfulness of the protagonists in his first three works, even though none is adolescent, strictly speaking. This observation is borne out by Delibes' sustained interest in the young in various later work, however, and in the aforementioned prologue to Volume Two of his *Complete Works,* the novelist identifies four constants or obsessive themes in his writing: death, childhood, nature, and the "Other." The first three are definitely of prime importance in *The Path,* and childhood and adolescence are treated extensively in *My Adored Son Sisí,* as well as in several novelettes and short stories, and one later novel, *The Rats.* Delibes also stated that he was particularly enthused with the idea of writing a novel about a child of three or four, a close observation of early childhood, which would attempt to demonstrate that at that age one lives in a fabulous world, very difficult to apprehend, but definitely existing.[7] Also in *The Path,* Nature looms very large, really coming to the fore for the first time, and the contact with death is one of young Daniel's most decisive experiences. Related to both Nature and death, the figure of the hunter also makes its initial appearance.

The first extensive use by Delibes of the "tag line," thenceforth something of a trademark of his style, is likewise found in *The Path.* Each character has a nickname, or a reference to his appearance, profession, or peculiarities, repeated with nearly every mention of his name. Daniel's nickname is "el Mochuelo," "the Owl," because of his solemn stare, and his friend Germán is "el Tiñoso," "mangy." Whenever the priest appears, the reader is reminded that Don José was "a great saint," and the name of Paco the Blacksmith is seldom invoked without his trade. In some cases, nicknames have displaced Christian or family names which may even be unknown. While this has been seen as an idiosyncrasy of Delibes and even considered a stylistic abuse,[8] it is also an aspect of realism. In remote villages such as he treats, it is not uncommon for most inhabitants to be related, so that use of a family name may not identify sufficiently. Therefore, the trade or profession may be used to distinguish, or a nickname. Use of the first name or nickname is characteristic, too, of children and adolescents, and logical in a work whose principal characters are of this age. First-name usage is frequent in the face-to-face relationships of rural areas and small towns, as well. Whether or not Delibes abuses repetition of tag-lines and nicknames is a question of individual taste; however, it should be remembered that part of his purpose is humor, and part recreation of the village atmosphere, both of which ends are served by this repetition.

Another technique employed extensively by Delibes for the first time in *The Path* is caricaturization. Many characters are presented only in certain rather narrow dimensions, usually with two or three outstanding traits or quirks, often exaggerated, mentioned whenever the character appears. This has the limitation of not allowing psychological profundity, but is a useful device for differentiating characters, especially when many are treated in a relatively short space. The use of caricature by Delibes has also been condemned by hostile criticism,[9] but it is a legitimate literary technique and he handles it well. The fact that characters so sketched may be conceived with irony does not justify the allegation that Delibes treats his fictional creatures with indifference and contempt. On the contrary—and many observers have noted this—he feels considerable tenderness for most of his characters, as well as for their real-life prototypes. This does not exclude a clear vision of their weaknesses, or a touch of irony about their quirks and manias; neither does it constitute scorn.

Daniel's best friend is Roque, something of a bully and know-it-all, two years older, who reveals to "el Machuelo" and a third boy, Germán, many of the mysteries of life and death, and in particular, unveils the secrets of "that"—reproduction, birth, and sterility. Roque is the son of Daniel's hero, Paco the blacksmith, a widower, quarrelsome drunkard, and supposedly the greatest sinner in the area. Paco's strength is a local legend, and once during Holy Week he carried unassisted the image of the patron virgin, allegedly over two hundred kilos with its litter. (The patroness of Molledo-Portolín, the village which served as model, is Nuestra Señora del Camino, an image set in the exterior wall of the local church, and possibly of some significance in relation to the title.) Daniel's idea of greatness is to emulate Paco, and he cannot quite comprehend his parent's other ambitions for him.

The village, in comparison with those of the Castilian plateau to the
south described in Delibes' later works, is probably less backward and
poor; it is set in a lush, green, well-watered valley, and no one appears
hungry. The main interest is not the epic of hunger and the struggle for
survival against an implacable Nature, as for example in *The Rats* or *Old
Tales of Old Castile,* but in the characters, whose small adventures and
misadventures acquire sharper relief against the monotony of their daily
existence. One such episode concerns Sara, the fearsome old maid sister
of Roque. She first appears as a religious fanatic, whose pastime and
solution to all problems is reciting the rosary for the dead. Because she
punished Roque by making him participate, Daniel and the two friends
scheme to distract her attention permanently. While there is no
statement that Sara's attitude is a sublimation of frustration, the boys
intuitively choose the proper cure: the shy schoolmaster begins to
receive notes signed with her name, while the repressed Sara is the
recipient of written advances supposedly signed by him. This strategem,
after some setbacks, finally leads to matrimony.

There are two other sets of pious old maids in the village, the three
sisters known as the "Guindillas," "hot peppers," because of their long,
straight bodies, ruddy complexions, and fiery dispositions, and the five
"Lepóridas," so denominated because all resemble rabbits. Among the
breaks in the even tenor of village life, the second Guindilla dies, the
third runs away with a bank clerk who lasts exactly as long as her
money, and the eldest eventually marries the widowed, one-armed
saloonkeeper, each with appropriate humorous and intimate detail
known to the entire hamlet.

During the narration, the reader becomes acquainted with most of
the edifices in this microcosm, the wooden houses with their open
balconies painted blue and filled with geraniums, the nail factory, the
empty mansion of the local noble, the city hall, the Guindillas' general
store, an inn, the main square with its public fountain, a tiny branch
bank, the estate of the local *indiano* (one who has made a fortune in
America), the smithy, the telephone office (operated by the Lepóridas),
a bazaar, the priest's house and the church, the school and master's
quarters. Except for a few houses not individually identified, there is
little else. Each building has its history, some anecdote connected with
either the road or railroad, the only links with the outside world. As it
is only in this other world that time as the twentieth century knows it
exists, these two lines of communication also acquire undertones of
time symbolism.

Although it is repeatedly reiterated that Don José, the priest, was a great saint, it is true as Hickey notes that there is no evidence of sanctity.[10] It seems excessive, however, to call Delibes anticlerical, as this critic does, even though most priests portrayed by the novelist are not flawless. But Don José is not presented negatively in his relationship to the villagers, even though most of his sermons concern violations of the Sixth Commandment (by Spanish count, the prohibition of lust). While apparently moved by generous offerings to respond with longer prayers, Don José is not presented as a hypocrite or sinner, and the worst that can be said is that he is somewhat narrow in his moral criteria and perhaps overly simplistic in his theology. On the other hand, a more sophisticated approach would not reach the villagers. Simply because Delibes does not idealize the representatives of the Church (in itself part of realism) is insufficient grounds for charging anticlericalism.

Another interruption in the monotonous passage of time, of more transcendent significance for Daniel, is the accidental drowning of his friend, Germán. A rather sickly boy, Germán was extremely fond of wild birds, and a disease contracted from them resulted in losing parts of his hair, the cause of his nickname ("mangy"). After Germán's death, Daniel killed a thrush and put it surreptitiously in the coffin. When discovered, as he fearfully denied knowledge of the matter, it was considered a miracle by the superstitious villagers, although Don José obviously suspected the truth. Germán's death, some four weeks before Daniel's scheduled departure for the city, signified an end to childhood, the first rupture of a heretofore idyllic existence which would be definitively terminated by his leaving the valley.

As noted in the introduction to the edition for American students,[11] the underlying "problem of the direction a man should give to his life" is the theme of *Still It Is Day;* this is equally applicable to *The Path* for it is a basic preoccupation in each of Delibes' first three novels, although the attitudes of the protagonists with respect to the problem vary enormously. Daniel's wish not to "progress" is almost the opposite of Sebastián's attitude, but there are considerable differences in age and other vital circumstances.

Delibes has suceeded fairly well in eliminating himself as narrator or consciousness from the pages of *The Path,* and in presenting events from the protagonist's viewpoint, a technique henceforth employed frequently. However, there are some comments unjustified by the experience of an eleven-year-old, as well as statements attributed to other characters which are too literary or erudite in vocabulary to belong in the mouths of rude villagers. Most of these, though, occur in passages of a humorous nature, involving exaggeration, and it is possible that the novelist deliberately inserted out-of-character remarks for the sake of humor. In any case, these inconsistencies are not too numerous, and in context, not jolting for the reader. Another possibly unrealistic element is that some acecdotes took place before the birth of Daniel, or when he was two years old, so that he cannot really remember them. However, they form part of the local tradition, and as one of the few available amusements is storytelling, the boy would obviously have heard each episode repeated many times. Then, too, the novelist could have crowded the events into a shorter time, but has deliberately refrained from doing so in order to better reproduce the static, timeless nature of life in the village. The retrospective technique employed is particularly suited for this purpose, minimizing the sense of action, as does the structure, wherein plot is nearly eliminated.

Delibes felt a special fondness for this village, and undoubtedly during his boyhood summers had himself lived some of the adventures of Daniel. His youngest daughter is named María del Camino, after the village's patron virgin. The use of caricature in the novel may be a defense against sentimentalizing; in any case, with Delibes it is not cruel or sarcastic, but a gentle, smiling irony. Nor is life in the countryside idealized, for even if it is a refuge from mechanization and the negative side of civilization, it is also remote from the positive content of progress, which the novelist quite clearly realizes. *The Path*, perhaps in part because of its setting, differs from many twentieth-century novels of adolescence in the more positive and innocent portrayal of the protagonist, and in that the discovery of life's mysteries does not provoke a psychological crisis, premature debauchment, or disillusionment. It has been suggested that the difference may be due to the relatively tender age of Daniel, or to the fact that Delibes treats not a single child but a little band of three. In any case, Delibes' work implies that it is still possible to enter adolescence without serious trauma, at least in the remote and rather pastoral environment selected. While some critics objected that this was excessively idyllic, it is obvious that many readers liked to believe that such innocence is still possible, and this, perhaps more than any other aspect of the novel, accounts for the overwhelming success of *The Path*.[1][2]

CHAPTER 4

The Anti-Malthusian Thesis

D ELIBES' fourth novel, *Mi idolatrado hijo, Sisí (My Adored Son Sisí),*[1] is considered by some his most ambitious work, and this is certainly true of the time spent writing it, and of its length, some three hundred densely printed pages. It is likewise ambitious in the period it spans, some thirty years ending with the Civil War. Only his first novel covers a comparable period of time, and if *The Cypress* may be said to be more ambitious geographically, *Sisí* is more so historically, recreating an epoch in the life of Valladolid. Judging by the intent or purpose of the various works, however, *Sisí* is relatively more limited in scope, for the novelist has stated on several occasions that he wrote this work "to combat Malthusianism." Thus, this is definitely a thesis novel, and is so identified by Delibes. However, it involves no preaching or overt statement of the thesis; the novelist allows the reader to draw his conclusions from the facts presented (although, of course, the facts are so arranged as to lead to certain conclusions). This, indeed, is the basis distinction between a thesis novel and propaganda, and in accord with Delibes' stated principles: "I only accept the thesis novel when this (the thesis) derives from the facts themselves, without admonishing or preaching."[2]

Perhaps testifying to the skill and success of the novelist in masking his thesis is a review of *Sisí* by a Catholic critic who expressed doubt that Delibes had a thesis, while concluding that the novel showed the consequences of badly educating one's children. It was his opinion that the novel did not pursue any specific moral end.[3] This observer classified the novel as a combination of the psychological and the naturalistic, believing the author's purpose to be the analysis of egotism. Others who suggested that it was, indeed, a thesis novel, did not agree as to what the thesis might be, despite clear clues given by the novelist at the beginning: He dedicates the work to his seven brothers and sisters each by name, and prefaces the novel with a passage from the Book of Genesis, the command to "be fruitful, multiply and replenish the earth."

It will be remembered that Malthus theorized that when civilization reached a certain level, the earth's population would increase geometrically; foreseeing the inevitable "population explosion," he was among the early advocates of birth control. Most readers will be aware that the Catholic Church took a strong, dogmatic stand against this, and that in Latin countries its position was buttressed by cultural elements, a predominant tendency to judge masculinity in proportion to the number of offspring, and a system of life still fundamentally patriarchal. As an orthodox Catholic and one raised in a large family, himself the father of seven children, Delibes obviously accepted the Church's posture. One might speculate that if his experience had been in the lower classes, where children of large families frequently do not have the necessities, he might have seen some virtue in Malthus' ideas. Perhaps he recognized this possibility but rejected it; in any case, the protagonist Cecilio Rubes expresses several variations of his notion that "Children are for the poor—they are accustomed to suffer."

In *Sisí* , Delibes presents a fundamentally vacuous, egotistical, and vulgar man who marries largely to satisfy his sensuality and his desire to flaunt the possession of a beautiful woman, not because of any interest in a family or domestic life. In fact, Cecilio Rubes makes having no children a prior condition to matrimony, a condition accepted by his wife Adela, terrified of childbirth because her own mother died when she was born. By the second year of marriage, Cecilio also acquires a red-haired mistress, whom he sets up in an apartment overlooking the river. While his marriage is stale and his life routine, he apparently fails to notice that anything is lacking until after some seven years of marriage. Then, on Christmas Eve in 1917, as the novel opens, in an unaccustomed mood of sentimentality and depression, Cecilio impulsively accepts his accountant's verdict that what he needs is a child. Inebriated, he demands one of his wife, who is already pregnant but afraid to tell him. Once Sisí is born, Cecilio wants no more children, both because he does not want the inconvenience and disturbance, and because he wishes the boy to have unlimited material benefits without having to share with siblings. Sisí is denied no whim, upon Rubes' orders; is even encouraged in willfulness and extravagance, and his mother's weak attempts to control him are countermanded by his father. By early adolescence, Sisí has fallen into bad company and acquired the vices of drinking, fornication, and smoking. His self-indulgence continues essentially uninterrupted until the Civil War, and Sisí, for whom no holds are barred, even has an affair with Paulina, his father's former mistress. However, he begins to suffer a premature tiredness of life, to drink too much, and undergo depressions. At the same time, he becomes interested for the first time in an innocent girl, but as he has never experienced a relationship based on anything but sexual attraction, believes he cannot be in love with her.

After being drafted and sent to an encampment in the country near the front, Sisí begins to realize the emptiness of his previous existence, and in contact with nature for a long period, to reflect upon the meaning of life. This process of "conversion" is reinforced when, on leave, he is even more seriously attracted by the girl next door, Elisa Sendín, one of a numerous family which in many respects offers a contrast or counterpart to that of Rubes. Influenced by her purity and religiosity, he decides to change his ways and goes to confession. The following day, having been transferred at his father's behest to a "less dangerous" zone farther from the front, he is killed tragically and ironically. Cecilio Rubes is unable to accept this reality, and after initial shock, blames his wife for the boy's death. After weeks of depression and self-pity, he demands another child of his wife, but she is too old. Then, feverishly, he takes his request to Paulina, only to learn that she is already pregnant—by Sisí. Despairing or crazed, Rubes throws himself from the balcony. His suicide, like his life, is implicitly selfish, materialistic, and weak. His manner of death has family precedents, for Cecilio's grandfather had thrown himself from the fourth floor into a stairwell. Rubes believed in family tradition, to the extent of using the shortcomings of his forebears to explain his own. Thus, his father was a drunkard, so Cecilio was not to blame for drinking too much. And while feeling occasional guilt for his marital infidelities, he excused himself by appealing to the "libidinous tradition of the family." The suicide is not too surprising as Cecilio has thought previously of this "solution" in moments of stress.

It is clear that *Sisí*, unlike its immediate predecessor, is a novel with a well-structured plot. Events for the most part follow an orderly chronological progression, with a few flashbacks of brief span and duration. Most of the narrative is third person, focussing alternately on Cecilio, his wife Adela, and Sisí, from whose viewpoints the corresponding sections are related. This is a variation on the technique of viewpoint developed in *The Path*, as the reader does not perceive everything through the eyes of one character. He has several perspectives, that of an impersonal narrator at the beginning, and then, in descending order quantitatively, that of Rubes, Sisí, and Adela—for despite the suggestion of the title, the principal character is not Sisí, but his father. Another (Dos Passian) technique frequently utilized by Delibes in *Sisí* is the interspersing of newspaper clippings, beginning with those dated December 24, 1917, to fix events clearly and firmly in their historical context. These excerpts of news and other announcements, ending with January 1, 1938, four days after the death of Sisí, taken from the files of *El norte de Castilla,* recreate as no fiction could the "feel" of the times. In the minute recreation of life in Valladolid (seen from the perspective of the bourgeoisie) during three decades, *Sisí* comes closer than any other work of Delibes to the historical novel, and could be placed in this category as legitimately as in that of thesis novel.

Actually, there are two faults or defects of Cecilio Rubes which act as prime determinants in the novel, seemingly omitted by the thesis as expressed, and which have their religious implications: selfishness and materialism. In a real sense, these are the disease, of which Rubes' "Malthusianism" is only a symptom. He has only one child because he is selfish and materialistic, not the other way around. Presumably the novelist intended readers to conclude, "If Cecilio had had more children, they could have consoled him at the death of Sisí," but it is difficult to imagine such an empty, egotistical personality being truly happy, or to care much if he is not. Many readers must have censured Rubes more for his selfish materialism than for having only one child, or for that matter, for idolizing him (although theologically, idolatry is a graver sin). So analyzed, the thesis becomes even more limited than the author believed, for he has not combatted Malthusianism per se so much as a selfish or materialistic refusal to have children when one has no economic hindrance.

Despite his defects, and even though Delibes may have originally intended otherwise, Rubes is by far the most interesting character, and his son a rather pale reflection who occupies less space and arouses less interest. From the reader's point of view, Sisí never becomes much more than a victim of the way in which he has been raised. Cecilio, on the other hand, holds more fascination because he is more complex, more autonomous, and more reprehensible. Sisí is never exposed to consistently positive influences until close to the end of the novel, and almost immediately reacts favorably. Previously, there had been only inconsistent and abortive attempts at discipline by his mother, cancelled by his father's intervention, or overshadowed by the stronger pull toward premature debauchment exercised by his juvenile associates. Shortly before his death, and as a result of his contact with nature and Elisa, Sisí has apparently repented, and although the pull of his former habits is strong, attempts to change for the better. According to the priest who heard his confession the day before, he, Sisí, "had excellent intentions." However, as his death came before he could put these into effect, he falls into the "faith without works" classification into which Hickey puts many of Delibes' characters.[4] Whether this will suffice to save him or not, the novelist does not presume to say. The father, however, is eternally condemned by his suicide, from the orthodox Catholic point of view.

While *Sisí* is not a novel that defies classification, it can be made to fit a number of molds. The novelist, in reply to the criticism by Cerezales cited earlier, retorted that it was a "Catholic book that teaches a moral."[5] However, Hickey, who sets forth the criteria for the "Catholic novel," decides that *Sisí* is not one, despite acknowledging that Delibes is combatting Malthusiansim in the name of Catholicism.[6] It could equally well be considered a historical novel or thesis novel, and the critic previously cited called it psychological and naturalistic. There is still another view, according to which it is a "social novel."[7] This investigator makes a convincing case for his classification on the grounds that *Sisí* is an exposé of the *dolce vita* of the bourgeoisie. But since the novelist has not included this novel in the volume of "social" narratives in his *Complete Works,* giving it a different classification, it seems (with the numerous possibilities) that Delibes' statement of intent should be considered. Thus, *Sisí* would be primarily a Catholic and moralizing thesis novel.

Cecilio Rubes is the millionaire proprietor of a plumbing establishment, dealing largely in appliances for the bath, apparently something of a luxury at that time in Valladolid. In his Dos Passos style-documentation of the history of the epoch, Delibes includes among his news clippings many examples of commercial advertising of the period. The specific announcements for Rubes' firm are obviously fictitious, but pass almost unnoticed among the genuine. As Cecilio inherited the business from his father, he has achieved but little in life, and his one claim to distinction is the invention of a special bathtub designed for the overweight (inspired by his own portly physique). He imagines that this contribution to civilization at least rivals the discoveries of Pasteur or the Curies, but nobody buys it. His invention has been called "the symbol (and perhaps the only real symbol in the book) of his useless life."[8] Whether or not Delibes intended this symbolism, the empty prototype of Cecilio's invention does indeed summarize his existence: pretentious, inane, and vacuous.

My Adored Son Sisí has not equalled the popularity of *The Path* with the public, although certain critics prefer it. Despite the technical similarities with Dos Passos,[9] it is essentially traditional in form, quite fully in the novelistic tradition of the past century. Of all the works of Delibes, perhaps this one most resembles Galdós, with whom the present-day novelist has also been compared. Insofar as both are realists, with some coincidence in moralizing or critical intent, there is a certain basis for comparison, but it is not a comparison based on specifics. And in general ideology, the two are quite different.

Although many critics were to see the fourth novel as a step backward in stylistic development, *Sisí* continues the process of search and experimentation which began with Delibes' first works. Despite some similarities in style, it is quite different from the first two novels, and a complete change of pace from *The Path*. All autobiographical content has been eliminated, except for what may be present in the background (Valladolid), and insofar as it is a thesis novel, *Sisí* is a thoroughly self-conscious work, which the three previous efforts were not. Delibes called his first three novels the fruits of intuition, but the presence of a thesis requires a degree of awareness that purely intuitive works would not attain. His future novels would also be very different in style, characters, tone, and ideology, perhaps justifying the notion that *Sisí* did not "belong" in Delibes' forward evolution, but nonetheless, *Sisí*, like the first two novels, reveals an essential dimension of Delibes—in this case, Delibes the moralist—without which acquaintance with his novelistic personality would not be complete.

CHAPTER 5

Short Stories and Novelettes

DELIBES' first piece of fiction was a short story, long since lost, though most of his published narrative efforts belong to the longer genres of the novelette and novel. However, he has stated that often his novels begin as short stories, that he first writes a short story and then develops it.[1] In other cases, short stories contain elements later incorporated in novels, not serving as the novelistic outline or skeleton but inspiring one incident of the whole. He also uses the short story to sketch a character later elaborated in a longer work. While Delibes' short stories are for the most part independent units which do not give the impression of being fragments of novels, they nevertheless have a close relationship to them in a number of cases.

Considering his more than twenty years as a narrator, Delibes has not published many short works, although some of them rival the longer fiction in excellence. *La partida (The Departure)*[2] is his first collection, ten stories of varying length, from a maximum of over forty pages to a minimum of eight. In addition, Delibes has produced a few other short stories scattered in various reviews, some of which are not easily available. These include "El recuerdo" ("The Memory"),[3] "La milana" ("The Hawk"),[4] "El amor propio de Juanito Osuna" ("The Self-Love of Juanito Osuna"),[5] "El conejo" ("The Rabbit"),[6] and "La barbería" ("The Barber Shop"),[7] this last published as a separate small booklet of sixty-four pages, three by four inches. Many of these individual stories appeared after the publication of *The Departure,* and it is likely that eventually they will be reedited, either in volume form, or in Delibes' *Complete Works.*[8] "El recuerdo," however, antedates *The Departure* by several years, and the failure to include it in that collection may indicate that the author did not intend to preserve it. It is one of his earliest works, whose composition must have coincided roughly with that of his first or second novel, and possibly he did not deem it worthy of preservation. On the other hand, it may have been

omitted simply because of the tonal or other difference from the rest of
the stories in the published volume.

Siestas con viento Sur (Siestas with the Southern Breeze)[9] contains
four narratives, "La mortaja" ("The Shroud"), "El loco" ("The
Madman"), "Los nogales" ("The Walnut Trees"), and "Los raíles"
("The Rails"). "El loco" and "Los raíles" were first published
individually in the undated "Novela del Sábado" series, and are
considerably longer than the other two works in this volume, which are
really merely substantial short stories. There is not a distinctly
perceptible geographical unity to the group, as might be suggested by
the title, although all can be presumed to take place in different areas
of Castile. Thematic coincidences are few. One unifying factor seems to
be psychological, insofar as each of the four works could be seen as a
study of a mental aberration, of a substandard or primitive mentality,
the elemental comprehension of a child, or the history of an obsession.
Unity, however, is not a prime factor. There are numerous differences
in style and intent, as well as tone and theme, but the collection
contains some of Delibes' best shorter works, and was distinguished by
the Spanish Academy's Fastenrath Prize. The two shorter pieces, which
will be called the short stories, are artistically superior to the novelettes
in this volume.

I La partida (The Departure)

The story which gives its title to the group and heads the collection,
also the longest of the ten, retells the first voyage of a young sailor. It
has been considered autobiographical by some commentators. However,
the autobiographical input is rather small, despite the fact that the
protagonist is named Miguel, is from Valladolid, and like the author,
has his first experience with the sea at approximately the age of
eighteen. The other circumstances of the fictitious Miguel are quite
different from those of his creator, and there are obviously literary
elements, including slight echoes of *The Cypress,* for like Pedro in that
novel, young Miguel has studied in the Naval School in Barcelona, and
is making a career of the Merchant Marine. Something of the same
symbolism is applied to the characters, with the idea of roundness
corresponding to an optimistic, cheerful disposition, and a long,
needle-like shape to the gloomy nature, in this case, the natures of mate
and engineer, respectively, of the vessel "Cantabria." The engineer has
the hobby of visiting cemeteries wherever his travels take him, and
Delibes himself once confessed to this habit. The young Miguel of the

story is an orphan, but has been raised by his mother's second husband as though he were a real son, even to the extent of sacrifices to help him study and launch him on his career. His adoptive father gave the boy his savings of three hundred *pesetas* to establish himself, which Miguel loses playing poker with the senior crew members his first night out.

"The Departure" has little other action, being largely an intertwining of Miguel's memories of Valladolid, and of his girlfriend Marita, mixed with incipient seasickness and nausea as a result of drinking in the mate's hot, filthy cabin. Delibes contrasts the role of "man of the world" which Miguel played with Marita, and his ingenuousness on the ship, as well as the differences between imagined first voyage and its reality. The clash between his romantic illusions and the rats, bed-bugs, and cockroaches which swarm over the "Cantabria" is effectively handled, as well as Miguel's nascent homesickness, the suspicion that perhaps he has made a mistake in the choice of career, and his reluctance to admit it. Technically, the work is twice retrospective, once covering the forty-eight hours in the "Cantabria" and again Miguel's previous life. Recent memories alternate with those of the period before embarcation. There are certain stylistic similarities with *The Path*, suggesting that "The Departure" may have been written at about the same time; the similarities involve particularly the forms of repetition, and the use of nicknames and tag lines.

"El refugio" ("The Shelter"), the second story of the collection, is much briefer, of some ten pages, and unlike most works of Delibes, directly reflects the Civil War. A thirteen-year-old boy recalls the behavior of various neighbors, mostly residents of the same apartment building, in a basement bomb shelter during the air raids. The action seems to take place shortly after the beginning of the war, and may well reflect a personal experience of Delibes, although the narrator is younger and probably more infantile than the author would have been at the same period. The story's theme is the refutation of the idea, apparently a popular saying, that danger creates bonds of solidarity. In any case, what the narrator recalls of the shelter is mostly a series of petty arguments, tiffs, and brawls, punctuated with resentments, and fear and hysteria which go unconsoled, causing amusement or satisfaction rather than sympathy in the others. One slightly macabre detail, perhaps related to an underlying moralizing intent, is that the shelter serves in normal times as a storehouse for coffins. This setting, combined with the danger motivating the characters' presence there, would imply that they would have done better to think on more transcendent matters than their petty squabbles.

"Una peseta para el tranvía" ("A Coin for the Streetcar") shows how a small coin can become a big problem when one does not have it. The anonymous protagonist has forgotten his wallet and has no money for the streetcar. It is raining, and he has promised "her," presumably a new love whom he hopes to conquer, to arrive early. Aware that she hates waiting, he vacillates between getting unromantically soaked by walking in the downpour and borrowing a *peseta* from an acquaintance. As he waits and no familiar faces appear, he suddenly remembers that in the next building, in a newspaper office, works a school friend he has not seen for over eight years. He decides to greet him and borrow the necessary coin, but in view of the other's effusiveness, is unable to state his true reason for the impromptu visit. Rather than confess, he spends over an hour as Luis shows him all the inner workings of the newspaper, and when he finally goes out, still without the coin, all traces of the rain have vanished.

"El manguero" ("The Hoseman") is primarily a character sketch of Tomás, a psychologically simple municipal employee whose main function is to water the plants in the park and to protect the flora and fauna. However, Tomás has no love for anything connected with his job, except that he enjoys overwatering saplings to the point of killing them, persecuting the birds, and fining little boys. He perversely soaks the benches daily just before the hour in which sweethearts congregate, savoring as one of his small satisfactions the sight of the girls leaving with wet dresses. His only other distraction is flirting with nursemaids who bring children to the park, even though Tomás is too old to interest these girls.

"El campeonato" ("The Championship") is one of the shortest of the collection, a sketch of the importance of soccer for the average Spaniard. Juan, the protagonist, spends the afternoon glued to the radio, ignoring the attempts at conversation of a frowsy blond girl who is presumably his mistress, and afterward, in a nearby bar, he talks of nothing but the recently completed game which had ended in a tie.

"El traslado" ("The Transfer") recounts the varying reactions of a man and his family when he is transferred by his company from Salamanca to the seaport and vacation resort of Santander. While his wife and six children anticipate pleasures and advantages because of the change, Blas thinks only of his propensity to colds and rheumatism. After the farewell banquet, however, in which he overeats and drinks and suffers an attack of nausea just when asked to speak, he begins to think that after all he could use a change of air.

"El primer pitillo" ("The First Cigarette") explores an extreme of sensual satisfaction. The nameless protagonist has just ended a two-week "fast," the result of an unexplained vow not to smoke for that period, and on the next morning converts the smoking of his first cigarette into an almost religious ritual of sensuality. "La contradicción" ("The Contradiction") is a change of pace, recounting the last moments of a boy who has been run over by a truck on the sidewalk. An adolescent of perhaps eighteen, he had just arrived in Valladolid with the purpose of getting work and "redeeming" his sister, a prostitute. Sor Matilde, a nun, suceeds in her effort to get him to repeat final words of repentance, overcoming his resentment at the truckdriver who, he believes, deliberately ran him down.

"En una noche así " ("On a Night like This") takes place on Christmas Eve, and there is an implicit comparison or contrast between the situation described and the first Christmas. The protagonist or central consciousness has just been released from prison, a physical wreck, suffering from rheumatism and a liver disorder; he is toothless at thirty years of age. Alone, with an empty stomach and little money, he encounters a beggar playing the accordion. The two of them talk and then find an out-of-the-way tavern about to close. In the locked establishment, they drink with the tavernkeeper, and each tells in fragments his personal tragedy, although the others are so preoccupied with their own that no one really listens. The tavernkeeper now suffers guilt over mistreating his pregnant wife, who was killed by a hit-and-run driver; the accordion player lost one eye and half his face when he was burned by the oil of a sidewalk doughnut-maker; and the ex-prisoner had turned to robbery to pay the doctor's bill after his son died during an operation and his wife disappeared. Each is spiritually alone, filled with bitterness and bewilderment, and with their physical and emotional mutilations, the three offer a grotesque parallel of the Three Kings. Probably it was not the author's purpose to suggest this parody, however, but to remind his readers of those who are unhappy and suffering at Christmas time. There is some possible autobiographical basis, insofar as Delibes had a good deal of contact with those released from the various prisons around Valladolid in the years following the Civil War. He did his best to help those coming out to find work and reestablish themselves, sometimes at considerable personal risk.

"La conferencia" ("The lecture"), the last tale in the collection, like the previous one takes place on a bitterly cold winter evening. José, whose wife Elvira works out, does not wish to go home until after eight because the place will be cold, and so in search of warmth enters a building where there is a lecture on Economics, "The Redistribution of Income." There is irony throughout, because José represents those who should be most interested in such redistribution, but cares only for the radiator, while the most avid member of the audience is an upper-class girl who is present only because she is an intellectual snob. The lecturer's thoughts reveal his total lack of interest in his own subject, but a considerable preoccupation with the hips of the girl in the front row.

The unity of this collection is rather nebulous, but it seems that most of the stories have a common setting, for the most part Valladolid, with one or two involving characters from that city in other parts (as in the title story), or set in nearby areas of old Castile. Also, most story situations are either related to Delibes' personal experience, verifiable from his biography, or are things which he had occasion to observe firsthand. In other words, they are stories with a minimum of invention or "fiction," told for the most part with few literary pretensions, and in a minor key. Stylistically they show some irregularities, probably reflecting different times of composition, but the most consistent aspects are the use of repetition and the "tag line." With the possible exception of "The First Cigarette" and perhaps "A Coin for the Streetcar," the protagonists are lower-class, humble people, and rather elementary in their psychology and reactions. The general tone is slightly ironic, occasionally critical, and in a few cases, implicitly moralizing. None of these aspects are significantly different to permit general statements as to variation or dissimilarity between the short stories and Delibes' longer works, except for the obvious disparity of length itself.

II   The Barbershop

Published as a wallet-size book, *The Barbershop* is really a short story, beginning with a quotation from Einstein to the effect that the pipe is as useful to civilization as the atomic bomb, if neither is used too much. The general purpose of the story is to show the importance of the small, everyday things, while suggesting that with excessive use, these can acquire the destructive characteristics of a bomb, in their limited sphere. The tale is told from the perspective of Don Floro

Domínguez Vaquero, a wealthy, lifelong client of Julio Alvarez. The story begins at the moment that Julio has informed Don Floro that he is going to sell his barbershop, as he has grown old and the business is no longer profitable. This provokes, by association, recollections of Don Floro beginning in childhood, when going to the barbershop had already begun to assume for him the proportions of a vice. Unlike other boys, he never had to be told to keep still, as a haircut for him was an extremely sensual experience. When asked what he wanted for his birthday, he chose an entirely superfluous haircut.

Upon inheriting his parents' holdings, he rapidly ran through the lands, but kept those properties "on paper" (presumably securities), as he cared only for what he could hold in his hand. Don Floro never worked in his life, or did anything useful that the reader can detect; he lived exclusively for that day every two weeks when he could go the barbershop. He simply wasted the rest of his life, alternating between his club, where his activity was limited to reading newspapers, and home, where he took a siesta from 4:00 to 9:00 P.M., thereafter going out again until 4:00 A.M. His life was regulated by a "British" valet, Walter (really Spanish, since no authentic import was available). Don Floro had only one "love" although to judge from the description, not much passion existed on either side: he once seized her hand in pretended emotion and was slapped in return, eventually breaking with her because she wanted him to wear long hair, the fashion during the reign of Amadeo. Since this would have meant sacrificing his periodic visits to the barbershop, Don Floro sacrificed her instead. Most of the events of the latter half of the nineteenth century are witnessed by Don Floro from inside the barbershop, a tumultuous period politically, but wherein he worries only about not having his barber's ministrations interrupted. Thus, his life's only outburst of passion occurs moments after the outbreak of a "revolution," scolding the barber whose attention was momentarily distracted.

Don Floro, during the years, is shown as aware of what is happening in the world only insofar as it is discussed in the barbershop. Life passes by without touching him; apprentice barbers marry, become fathers, grow older, one wife dies, and Don Floro is unaware, until receiving the earthshaking news of Julio's intent to sell. His one reason for existence now destroyed, he goes home to bed, makes his will, and dies, leaving five thousand *duros* to his valet, a locket containing his hair to the former sweetheart, and the bulk of his fortune to Julio, on the condition that he make no change in the barbershop and not cease to operate it during his lifetime. In showing how small and routine acts can become an overpowering vice, this story is thematically related to "The First Cigarette."

III *Miscellaneous Short Stories*

"El recuerdo" ("The Memory"), published in 1949, and probably composed at approximately the same time as the first novel, is a tale whose protagonist has a philosophy resembling that of Pedro in that novel. What he considers the necessity of preserving his innate automony, his freedom, leads him to break deliberately with his fiancée, in the belief he can triumph only without the burden of a wife. Twenty years later, alone on Christmas Eve, he drunkenly recalls the end of that relationship, the beginning of a loneliness now almost intolerable. Continuing to drink, he comes to associate the obsessive memory of that scene with his dog, Godoy, at the same time that the feeling of isolation increases. Foggily blaming the dog, he ends by shooting the faithful mastiff, his only companion. The style of "El recuerdo" is very different from that of the mature Delibes, rather verbose by comparison. While the story is interesting, what is not too convincing is the abrupt transition from what is defined as a true love situation to the decision to break with Julia.

"La milana" ("The Hawk"), published in 1963, has as its protagonist Azarías, a humble, uneducated, simpleminded, and rather elderly man, employed for minor menial tasks by an Extremaduran gentlemen. His family and employer seemingly have indifferent relationships with him, not unpleasant, but not close. His one weakness is the "Milana," an enormous captive owl-hawk, for which he cares as for a baby, even stealing small game birds from the master's hunting bag to feed to the Milana. Azarías is unable to count beyond eleven and is an extremely elementary being, comparable to tío Ratero in *The Rats*. He lives in unusually close contact with nature—birds seem more real to him than people. "The Hawk" is probably related in inspiration to "The Self-Love of Juanito Osuna," published in the same year, and among the few tales set outside Castile (both in Extremadura). Both could be classed as experimental, but while "The Self-Love" is implicitly a dialogue, a second-person monologue, "The Hawk" is third person, with only indirect dialogue, told from the viewpoint of a far more primitive mentality. Both are extremely colloquial, but in one case it is the language of the aristocracy, in the other, that of the lower class.

Both are essentially conversational, with a good deal of repetition and long, rambling constructions. In "The Hawk" Delibes employs an unusual number of "ands," "buts, " and "thens," to give the flavor of what the story would be as orally narrated by Azarías.

The great owl-hawk sickens at an advanced age, and Azarías, weeping frantically, begs the *señorito* to call a local wise man, but his request is ridiculed and the bird dies. Azarías places the body inside his shirt and goes to his sister's, where he and the youngest boy bury it. After the "funeral," he notices something about the child that reminds him of the owl-hawk, and begins to caress the boy in the same fashion as he used to smooth the bird's feathers.

"The Self-Love of Juanito Osuna" is technically and artistically one of Delibes' best achievements in the short story, a culminating point of his narrative technique. In this long monologue (or conversation with mute interlocutor), a fanatic amateur hunter, Paquito, discusses the defects of his "friend" Juanito, unwittingly revealing his own greater shortcomings. The technique resembles that employed in the novel, *Five Hours with Mario,* and this story may have been composed shortly before the longer work. In both, Delibes analyzes a character by means of reminiscences about another who does not appear. Aside from the self-deception in both cases and the fact that two personages so completely given to criticizing others see only virtue in themselves, the similarities are largely technical and stylistic. The short story is told in colloquial, conversational language, with considerable repetition, although here the "tag line" is not used. There is a similar device, as Paquito repeats certain affirmations over and over with little or no variation, but nicknames as such are not employed.

Paquito, apparently a wealthy landowner from Extremadura (judging from his associates), is entertaining a guest after a hunt in which both have participated. As they await the serving of the evening meal, Paquito monopolizes the conversation, vivisecting all others who had taken part in the hunt, but especially Juanito Osuna, who had bagged the most partridges. While insisting that Juanito is his best friend, that Juanito would do anything for him, and that he is a marvelous person, Paquito repeats obsessively that Juanito suffers from the defects of pride and self-love, and that he is "completely crazy." Juanito's madness seems to consist primarily in lording it over Paquito whenever he bags more game, and while Paquito insists that he hunts only for the exercise and fresh air, it is obvious that he is unnerved by the other's success. As the monologue continues, he says the same thing about every other person he mentions: that the person is completely crazy. This quite naturally tends to make the reader doubt that judgment, the more so as the proof is less and less convincing. In the final case, Paquito affirms that one of his shepherds is quite insane because he saves wool to make mattresses for his daughters when the five of them marry. Such "insanity" indicates that, for the aristocrat, being crazy consists of doing anything he criticizes, even when in another frame of reference it could be perfectly normal and even laudable.

There are strong social undertones to the story as Paquito, his friends, and interlocutor all appear to be of the upper class. There is a possibility, however, that the interlocutor is Delibes himself; in any case, with his long hunting experience, he must have met more than one personality like Paquito, and others like Juanito Osuna and the rest of the party described. Hunting is not the main theme, even though it seems to occupy all the space and all of the narrator's attention. Rather, this is a story somewhat in the vein of *The Barbershop,* insofar as it reveals the worthless existence of the bourgeoisie, theirs being an idle and parasitic way of life. This has not even produced interesting personalities but monomaniacs, men whose single vice makes them crashing bores. It is clear, too, that Paquito is a social snob, as he mentions the titles and wealth of each of the hunters, dwelling upon the fashion in which each has thrown away a fortune. The mention of the poor and frugal shepherd is an eloquent contrast, and the lack of sensitivity with which Paquito dismisses the shepherd's saving for his daughters' future is one of the story's most subtle touches. "The Self-Love of Juanito Osuna" may well be one of Delibes' strongest social indictments, despite the understated tone and indirect present-ation. Quite unaware that he is doing so, Paquito dissects the Extremaduran aristocracy, the leisure class to which he himself belongs, exposing the falseness and pettiness of their existence. The story is extremely ironic, without its tone being so, and the result can be counted among Delibes' best artistic achievements.

IV   Siestas con viento Sur
(Siestas with the Southern Breeze)

There seems to be no special rationale for the ordering of the four narratives in this volume, except that there is an alternation of length: short story, novelette, short story, novelette. Each employs the technique of the viewpoint in a different way; the author as narrator is not visibly present in their pages. The settings are rather difficult to localize, although each is obviously different. The two short stories, "The Shroud" and "The Walnut Trees," takes place in what is apparently the Castilian countryside, and the two novelettes, "The Madman" and "The Rails," in a city, which in the latter case is definitely indicated to be Valladolid by auto licenses. "The Rails" is subtitled "Outline for a Novel," although it is difficult to imagine that this particular situation could offer much more potential than that already exploited.

"The Shroud"[10] is narrated from the viewpoint of a small boy known only by his nickname, "el Senderines," a motherless child despised by his father, Trino, because he shows no sign of developing the latter's brute force. The setting is a semidesert area, a barren river valley unpopulated except for a hydroelectric plant and factory, with the huts of the workers nearby. Trino neglects Senderines, who essentially raises himself, trying with scant success to fulfill the one paternal demand: to show no fear. The action commences one Saturday evening with the arrival of Trino, who drunkenly falls unconscious and nude on the bed. At nightfall, when the child can no longer continue playing in the mud, he enters and finds his father dead. Senderines is obsessed by the obligation not to fear, as a last filial gesture, and the duty to dress Trino's body before any of the neighbors see him. The story centers on his futile efforts to clothe the body, weighing more than one hundred kilos, and this failing, to obtain help, as it becomes increasingly urgent for him to have Trino dressed before daylight.

From the nearest neighbor, Goyo, he learns the probable cause of Trino's death. The two had spent the afternoon in a tavern with other workers, where Trino argued with Baudilio over which could eat more. He consumed two dozen eggs, a whole roast suckling pig, and two liters of wine to win the dispute. Goyo refuses to help Senderines, because while playing cards, Trino had struck him and Goyo had sworn never to help him again, dead or alive. He insists that this oath is sacred. Conrado, who soothes the boy somewhat, is likewise unable to help as he is on duty at the power plant and cannot leave. Wandering in the darkness, the child encounters "el Pernales," a vagabond who comes each summer and breaks rocks by the river. "El Pernales" extorts from the boy a promise to give him his father's shoes and new suit before agreeing to help, and once in the hut, manages to get the stockings, Sunday shirt, and other garments of the deceased. When he threatens to leave the boy alone with the body at 2:00 A.M., Senderines offers him almost all that remains if he will stay until six o'clock, including the radio and alarm clock and the remaining clothes. Then the child falls asleep, and when he wakens, Conrado is there.

"El Senderines" is a probable prototype of "el Nini," child protagonist of *The Rats*.[11] While Senderines is less fully developed, they share numerous traits. Both have lost their mothers, and their fathers are animalistic (more so in the case of "el Nini"). Each boy essentially raises himself, living in close contact with nature, and faces responsibilities that should normally belong to adults. Both accept the state of affairs unquestioningly. The salient psychological traits of both child and father would seem to have been exaggerated in *The Rats*, as the boy acquires something close to clairvoyance and his progenitor has degenerated further to a moron or idiot.

"The Madman" is written in epistolary form, as the narrator addresses himself to the elder brother he has not seen since childhood. The letter, close to seventy pages, relates the solution of a mystery, complicated by the role of the unconscious. Almost twenty-five years previously, while still a small child, the narrator had witnessed the death of his father, supposedly a suicide, and had been found later crying hysterically, unable to speak. The elder brother ran away from home, never to return, while the younger remained with the mother until her death some two years before the narrative begins, at which point the narrator, Lenoir, has married and his wife is awaiting a child. In a bar, he hears a strange man telling the barman of his obsessive dream of being buried alive. Lenoir feels that this is something he has witnessed before, and is sufficiently intrigued to ask the waiter the man's name, which he is told is Robinet. In successive weeks, Robinet becomes an obsession for him, as he cannot shake off the conviction of having seen him before. His preoccupation and irritation cause him trouble at the bank where he works, and disputes with his wife; his mental state complicates his health, as he suffers from a ganglion and fever. The fixation increases, and almost deliriously he imagines the most improbable explanations, finally beginning to doubt his own sanity.

The narrator's father was an artist who had moved to Pau in the south of France with his wife and older son, where the younger boy was born. Lenoir has one of his father's paintings of Pau, and looking at it becomes convinced that it was there he first saw Robinet. Confined to his home because of the ganglion, he searches among other relics of his parents in the attic and finds a portrait of Robinet, painted by his father in Pau. As the doctor has recommended a change of climate, he decides to go there in search of Robinet. Once in Pau, many things begin to crowd his memory, and upon visiting the former residence he experiences a return to the past, becoming mentally the child of four who used to play on the stairway outside his father's studio and occasionally to peer through the keyhole. Upon looking once again, he relives the moment when he witnessed his father's death, as Robinet appeared in the skylight and shot him. Lenoir realizes he has finally made the link in his subconscious permitting him to reconstruct the repressed horror.

Returning to his boardinghouse, he finds Robinet in the elevator and knows that he is recognized when the latter says, "You have the same eyes as your father." Robinet insists that Lenoir and his wife accompany him, conducting them to a restaurant where he explains his killing of Lenoir's father. He repeats, with embellishments, the description of his obsessive dream of being buried alive which Lenoir first heard in the bar in Spain. Up to this point the story is well constructed, but it begins to falter, as apparently Delibes was unable to resolve it in these limits, so that Robinet ultimately reveals an Erostratus complex, the need to immortalize his name in order to live on in fame or infamy after his death, which makes the dream quite irrelevant. Having realized that he lacked the talent to become famous on his own merit, he recalls the example of Leonardo da Vinci and "la Gioconda," considering this a route to immortality. Admiring the work of Lenoir's father, he manages to meet him and commission a portrait, despite the artist's objection that he is not a suitable model. The first portrait does not satisfy Robinet, and he destroys it, obliging the artist to begin another. When he renounces the incomplete second attempt, Robinet decides to kill him, thinking that he can become famous also for having killed the painter who did not succeed in making him immortal, and that the matter would attract more attention if not explained until twenty-five years later. He then extends his written confession to Lenoir and shoots himself. Despite the narrator's disgust, Robinet indeed achieves a certain transient notoriety.

Except for the fact that the most significant "detective" work in this novelette is internal, within the narrator's subconscious memory, and with external "clues" functioning largely as a stimulus to recall, "The Madman" is very much within the tradition of the mystery story, a genre not frequently cultivated in Spain by the better writers. While it is in no way autobiographical, Delibes seems to have loaned "Lenoir" some of his own personal history. The "Lenoir" family began in Spain in the same fashion as that of Delibes, with the grandfather, an engineer, having come to supervise the building of the railroad between

Reinosa and Santander, and having met and married the grandmother in a village near a tunnel site. The employment in a bank, the ganglion, and the trip to the south of France are likewise taken from the novelist's own experience. The suspense of the tale is maintained until near the end, but despite considerable narrative interest, it is not typical of Delibes, nor is it one of his best works. While the psychology and mental search of the narrator are handled well, the motives of Robinet are less convincing. Even granting that he is mad, it seems something of an artistic error to have repeated the extended scenes concerning his fear of being buried alive when his real motivation is the overpowering desire for "immortality" in the memory of those who live after. This subject has no parallels in Delibes' work, and unlike most of his writing, "The Madman" is completely gratuitous, serving no purpose beyond itself.

"The Walnut Trees," is one of the most characteristic tales of Delibes, very much in the vein of *The Rats* and other works on Castile. The protagonist, Nilo the younger, is a deformed mongoloid with a cleft palate, the last of six sons of Nilo the elder, all named Nilo. The other five had died shortly after birth. Nilo the elder tells his wife that the sixth also dies, rather than reveal his deformities, and although the unfortunate child lives, his mother dies before seeing him. Nilo the elder, once rich, has been forced by years of famine to sell his remaining land, and is left with only some beehives and six walnut trees.

Of all that he might have learned, only one thing impressed itself upon the mind of Nilo the younger, a remark by the schoolmaster that the work of God is perfect and man cannot improve upon it. This serves him as a rationale for almost total passivity, and he spends most of his time lying beneath the walnut trees, resisting his father's efforts to interest him in caring for them or the harvest. Nilo the younger does little in life but eat and sleep and scratch his feet. When the father has reached eighty and can no longer harvest his money crop of walnuts before they become the prey of birds, insects, and village boys, he once more tries to enlist the aid of Nilo the younger. Finding him asleep beneath the trees shortly after, Nilo the elder glumly ascends the first tree and begins to work. Neither this nor his activity awakens Nilo the younger, not even the impact of the old man's body falling beside him.

"The Rails" is something of a literary spoof, a semi-serious investigation of hereditary determination. Actually there are two parallel narratives, the histories of two Timoteos, one the grandfather of the other. The older was Teo, the younger is Tim. Each fought in a war, Teo in the last of the Carlist Wars, and Tim in the Spanish Civil War. Each is summoned by his father after the close of hostilities and told to choose a career, and each chooses against the father's judgment. The respective fathers die shortly after these scenes, and each son swears at graveside to succeed. Tim is unaware of these events in his grandfather's life, some eighty years previous, and although they are like "two rails," he does not know it. Like Teo, he has little will, but imagines that he is indomitable. Teo, the grandfather, was a waiter whose ambition was to become a *maître,* while Tim studied law and spent twelve years preparing himself for *oposiciones,* public examinations for various government positions in the legal field. Unsuccessful in seven attempts, he becomes a hopeless perpetual student. Tim has no ability to synthesize the information he memorizes, as his ancestor was unable to put to use the English he attempted to learn from an ancient grammar, imagining that the railroad would bring tourists and create a market for his talent. Teo spent his entire life as a waiter, with a wife who threatened infidelity, solving his domestic arguments by the threat to commit suicide by cutting his wrists (which he never does because he is afraid of blood). One of his grandsons, Tim's supposedly abnormal brother Ramón, does kill himself in exactly this manner at the age of seventeen. Like Teo, Tim is repeatedly unsuccessful, and his girlfriend betrays him. Ultimately, however, he realizes that his endless studying has become a way of life, a habit which he cannot break without leaving an unfillable void. Basically Tim does not wish to succeed, and drinks to celebrate his failure.

Structurally the tale alternates scenes from the two lives, separate in time but similar in the essentials. This is further emphasized by frequent use of repetition, with whole paragraphs sometimes repeated, while at other moments the same words are used by the two protagonists. To underline the sameness and monotony of their lives, the author also repeats the same scene several times in succession. The only difference is in the outcome, insofar as Tim realizes that he would not be happy being anything more than he is; the implication, however, is that he will spend his life studying to "get ahead" without doing so, just as Teo spent his years futilely with a similar dream. The "rails" may also signify the impossibility of turning around, of starting again, in addition to underlying the parallels in the two lives. Although the tone is occasionally somber, there is little serious content, with grim humor predominating. However, this work is probably the product of Delibes' interest in the effects of heredity, already explored somewhat in works such as *Still It Is Day* and *My Adored Son Sisí,* and to appear again in *The Rats.* There is a moment when the protagonist-narrator of "The Madman" thinks that the sensations provoked by Robinet are something inherited from his father, and while this is only a seemingly trivial passing thought, it serves to evince further the novelist's curiosity for genetic determinism, as do such cases as that of Nilo the younger and Tim's abnormal brother Ramón, both the sons of elderly men.

The novelettes, like the short stories, are stylistically comparable to Delibes' longer works. Of the four narratives in *Siestas with the Southern Breeze,* the two shorter ones, "The Shroud" and "The Walnut Trees," are fully within the vein of Delibes' most characteristic writings, while the more lengthy novelettes are somewhat lighter, seemingly lacking the attempted philosophical transcendence of his early novels, as well as the critical and social preoccupations of the later works. In its humor, use of repetition, and the caricaturesque traits of the two protagonists, "The Rails" has more formal resemblance to other works by Delibes than does "The Madman," although the latter's epistolary technique can be compared with the first-person narration of *The Cypress* or that of the two *Diaries* of Lorenzo. Delibes' constant themes are for the most part absent or submerged in the two novelettes, except for the theme of death and hints of his interest in heredity and the effects of early experiences upon psychological formation. Otherwise, the novelettes seem to have been written primarily for his own (and the reader's) amusement, rather rare in Delibes' writing. Aside from the relatively greater gratuity, *Siestas* may be more obviously related in inspiration to the longer works than the earlier collection of short stories, seeming to offer glimpses in miniature of principal characters or characteristics of the mature novels which were less clear or less significant than those contained in *The Departure.* This is especially true of "The Walnut Trees" and "The Shroud."

V   La mortaja (The Shroud)

Shortly after completion of the original manuscript of the present study, a new collection of short stories by Delibes was placed on the market. The title tale and longest narrative in this volume is exactly the same as that published earlier in *Siestas con viento Sur* and discussed above. There are eight additional titles in the new compilation, of which the second, "The Self-Love of Juanito Osuna," has likewise been treated already, together with the tales published in various reviews.

References to this tale in Miguel Angel Pastor's prologue to *The Shroud* indicate a basic agreement with the analysis made above, especially as regards social intent and the stylistic relationship to *Five Hours with Mario*. Of the seven titles remaining, "El conejo" likewise appeared previously in a periodical, but had not been discussed because of the difficulty of obtaining that particular number; thus, for reasons of convenience, it is studied with the other tales contained in *The Shroud,* several of which appear in print for the first time. The collection is definitely not a simple compilation of scattered tales previously published by Delibes, for not only does it contain considerable material unpublished before, but some stories already in print (such as "El recuerdo" and "La milana" discussed above) are not included.

A question logically arises as to the criteria of selection employed: it was obviously not completeness, unity of theme or setting, or recent chronology of composition (the time span is 1948-1963). The publisher's note on the back cover suggests an attempt at selection permitting acquaintance with the evolution of Delibes' work, exemplifying different themes, changes in style, and the two spatial axes of his work, the Castilian plain and the provincial capital. Whether this is a justification *a posteriori* or whether it did indeed serve as a prior rationale for an otherwise somewhat inchoate grouping is not entirely clear (and perhaps not too important).

There is another possible relationship among the tales in this collection, strongly implicit in the discussion by Pastor in the prologue. He tends to stress the germinal or nuclear nature of characters and situations with respect to longer works of Delibes. The novelist's own comments in this regard were cited at the beginning of this chapter (i.e., that he often sketched an idea in a short story, elaborating it in a novel). Pastor gives a brief resumé of Delibes' evolution, indicating progress toward an ever more strongly socio-critical posture, within an essential realism characterized by occasional touches of *esperpento*. (It becomes clear that this is given a specific and slightly unorthodox connotation, signifying Delibes' very personal use of caricature; thus in Pastor's essay the term lacks some of the moral and aesthetic implications given it by Valle-Inclán.)

While Delibes has more than once noted the embryonic nature of his short stories, Pastor has taken the affirmation more seriously than previous Spanish criticism, which has generally ignored the growing body of Delibes' shorter works (indeed, everything but his novels). This prologue is the first serious attempt by a Spanish critic to draw parallels or indicate possible connections between characters and situations in the brief narratives and those of like nature in Delibes' longer fiction. Some coincidences are fairly evident, and reiterate observations made earlier in this chapter, such as the related narrative techniques in "The Self-Love of Juanito Osuna" and *Five Hours with Mario,* and the fact that their apparently innocuous ambientation obscures a basically "social" (and hence political) nature. Pastor's observations of "El patio de vecindad" ("The Neighborhood Patio") while likewise fairly evident once one has access to the story, reveal a good knowledge of Delibes' works and a power of synthesis, as he related it in plot and theme to *La hoja roja (The Red Leaf).* While Pastor has not studied all of the points of contact or coincidence, his work is significant in being the only critical essay of any length devoted to Delibes' shorter narratives.

"The Neighborhood Patio" presents an old man, clearly similar to the retired Don Eloy in *The Red Leaf,* sharing the boredom of the person unemployed after long years of activity, the relative restrictions of those living on pensions, the timid fear of the world at large conflicting with a counterbalancing loneliness, memories of long-lost contacts, and a great power of illusion. Each has an almost obsessive hobby, in this case, the operation of an amateur shortwave radio set, which allows him some sort of "friendship" with other old and lonely people halfway around the world, and even the illusion of companionship, until one day, abruptly, he learns of the death of Doña Jacobita, a widow in Havana with whom he was accustomed to chat daily. The title has a double meaning, suggesting that the world (especially via shortwave) is just like a neighborhood backyard with its daily gossip. The old man, Don Hernando, used a sign warning "Danger of Death" to caution his young granddaughter not to touch the transmitter, and upon learning of the death of his faraway companion, symbolically places the sign on the set and turns it off. Even this sort of involvement carries the danger of death, of loss.

"El sol" ("The Sun") recalls technically the device used in "The Rails," characters with certain parallel traits. In this case, Delibes employs women with the same names, but of different social class. In fact, there are three pairs of names: the two female protagonists, Agueda (with various diminutives), their friends, Marifé (with variants of this name), and male suitors, Carmelo (or a nickname variant). The story ironically points up the different social values and connotations of a suntan versus paleness. The lower class women, employed to work on the road, attempt to keep their skin white (presumably in imitation of the middleclass housewife), veiling themselves in order to avoid acquiring a tan. Simultaneously, the others are seen at a nearby beach, going to ridiculous lengths to acquire as black a tan as possible. One of the greatest moments of irony comes when one of the vacationers points to the veiled roadworker and comments to her companion, "Really, we're nothing but Moors, there's no denying it."

"La fe" ("Faith") takes place in a hospital ward occupied by three women on the day of an important religious procession, each anxiously awaiting the moment when the saint's image will pass by the building in the hope of a miracle—for herself. The three characters are distinctly different, one extremely bitter, another married and preoccupied with her child (as well as both gratified and embarrassed by the presence of her husband), and an apparently senile old woman who constantly asks for a miracle (cessation of a nagging pain) and who convinces herself that she has received it at the moment the procession passes. The story contains several basic themes of Delibes: the lack of true charity (for each woman is essentially selfish in her "faith"), the different phenomena considered miraculous by the superstitious or naively religious in Spain (as in *Old Tales of Old Castile*), and the psychological process of self-deception—although he does leave unanswered the question of whether the "miracle" here is genuine, or whether the old woman has simply convinced herself that it happened.

"El conejo" ("The Rabbit") likewise involves a certain ironic parallel. There are two sicknesses and two deaths, two "funerals." One is that of a spinster who from excessive prudishness apparently prefers to die from an unidentified disease rather than undress in front of the doctor, and the rabbit belonging to a small boy which sickens because the child does not know how to care for it. The animal is killed by his elder brother, exemplifying a frequent and sometimes gratuitous cruelty in children, something of a constant theme in postwar Spanish writers. Both the spinster and the rabbit die because of a defective, ignorant treatment of matters related to their respective health, and are buried in similar ceremonies, as the boy is consoled by being able to play at conducting the funeral.

"La perra" ("The Dog") is apparently a hunting story, on its most superficial level, dealing with an incident when two hunters disagree as to the merits of a female hound belonging to one of them. While the owner defends her, his "friend" insists she is no good, and almost forces him to kill the dog (which he does) in order not to miss a shot at a rabbit when the dog is in the line of fire. Afterwards, the owner tries to credit the dead dog with having flushed out the prey, but his companion says he was busy with his own hunting and didn't see her. Actually, however, Delibes is concerned with the hunt only as a pretext for showing the lack of human warmth, sympathy, and understanding, even between "friends," and the gratuitous, sadistic cruelty with which the one man forces his companion to sacrifice the dog.

"Las visiones" ("Visions"), the tale which closes the collection, recalls "La milana" in technique and in the language, as well as the similar mentality of the central consciousness or protagonist, although in this case it is a woman of the lower class, an almost compulsive talker, who for half an hour stands explaining to some gentlemen from Bilbao just why her husband is not home when they had called the night before, advising that they would need his services as a hunting guide. Like "The Self-Love of Juanito Osuna" and "The Hawk" (as well as "The Dog"), this story is an example of how Delibes uses the ostensible theme of hunting as a point of departure for criticism of man's attitude toward his fellowman, sometimes basing the faults upon social inequities, sometimes upon personal defects. This monologue indirectly reveals the poverty and misery of the villager, a more or less innate stupidity in the speaker (increased and perpetuated by the environment), and is related to novels like *The Rats* in its exposure of the toll taken by residence in the backward villages. Technically, it is obviously related to "The Self-Love . . ." and *Five Hours with Mario,* although somewhat different stylistically because of the class and mentality of the speaker. Like most of Delibes' mature writings, it contains a notable amount of repetition and use of the tag line.

The Shroud is definitely one of Delibes' most important collections of shorter works, and with Pastor's helpful prologue, together with the varied selection, perhaps the one which gives the most complete idea of Delibes in the fewest pages. Despite the time range, the works chosen typify for the most part the mature Delibes, his more recent preoccupations, and in that sense are less an example of evolution than might be supposed. However, it does contain most of the constants of his narrative thematics, examples of several techniques, and excellent sections showing his mastery of popular speech. For the reader able to peruse only one short-story collection of Delibes, the choice should be *The Shroud.*

CHAPTER 6

The Diaries of Lorenzo

U NLIKE many contemporaries who have written trilogies or
novelistic cycles dealing with the same protagonist or core of
characters, Delibes has not until now attempted to write within a larger
narrative framework than the single novel. The two novels treated in
this chapter represent the only instance in which Delibes has repeated a
protagonist in a second work, the only case of a "sequel" or second
part to the adventures of one of his fictional creations. This, according
to the novelist's affirmation, was due to the extraordinary attraction
which the character of Lorenzo held for him. In the Prologue to
Volume Two of his *Complete Works,* Delibes explains that he sees
Lorenzo as "exemplary of the uncontaminated Spaniard, a product of
sun and wind, a braggart and yet controlled, long on talking and shorter
on deeds, vehement and dreamy, lazy and critical, but at the same time,
fair in love . . . noble in principles and loyal to his friends." [1]

For Delibes, Lorenzo as typically Spanish is necessarily extroverted,
which determined the choice of the diary form as the logical means of
his expression. "I see in him, when he hunts and when he loves, when
he works and when he dreams, a typically Hispanic manifestation. But
in order that he might be thus completely, it was imperative to give him
the faculty of exteriorization, that is, of speaking for himself,
directly." [2] The diary form was adopted because it offers a maximum of
freedom wherein the character may develop with a minimum of
structural and formal restraints. Delibes expresses the notion that
Spaniards may be identified not so much for what is said as how it is
said, and he considered the use of appropriate language in the two
diaries as one of their principal literary values. As Delibes points out,
the hunter, like many other specialized subspecies, has his own peculiar
language. Thus, in the case of Lorenzo, one finds not only the popular
speech of the man in the street, but the jargon of the hunt. So great was
the novelist's preoccupation with expression *per se* in these works that

he records his opinion that " . . .the real protagonist of my 'Diaries' is the language."[3]

One point raised repeatedly by critics concerned the verisimilitude of *Diario de un cazador (Diary of a Hunter)*, inasmuch as some questioned that such a completely ordinary character as Lorenzo would ever decide to confide his daily experience and impressions to a diary. The novelist replied that Lorenzo is not so ordinary, since he is a hunter—and the vanity of this breed often impels them to write of their venatic prowess. He does not find it unlikely, therefore, that Lorenzo should keep a diary, and feels that the only artifice, if any is involved, is that Lorenzo should decide to include not only matters of the hunt, but also his professional and sentimental affairs.

The *Diaries* are among Delibes' favorites within his own production, being works in which he freely expressed his own passion for hunting, and was able to indulge his fascination with the language. It may be for these reasons, as well as because of the attraction exercised by the character of Lorenzo, that Delibes wrote the second novel. While some commentators accused him of wishing to capitalize on the overwhelming success of the first *Diary*, not necessarily reprehensible in itself, Delibes has denied this imputation. He has stated on several occasions that the character of Lorenzo continues to intrigue him and that there is a strong possibility that he may one day send him on further adventures.

I   Diario de un cazador
(Diary of a Hunter)[4]

The dedicatory prologue contains a few personal and autobiographical notes, revealing primarily the conditions under which Delibes is accustomed to hunt and the type of people encountered. The work is dedicated to his father, still an active hunter at the age of eighty (and alive when the work was published), and the other members of his *cuadrilla*, the group with which Delibes customarily hunted. Except for the *Complete Works*, Delibes has seldom prefaced his work with personal statements, but the fact that they are found before both *Diaries* is a logical indicator of the degree of the novelist's personal involvement. These companion volumes, and particularly the first, denote Delibes' mastery of his own characteristic style, the tone and thematics which mark his works of maturity.

Diary of a Hunter was awarded the National Literary Prize for 1955, and some critics gave it their vote later on as "Book of the Year." One observer called it "the first and only neo-realist novel written in Spain,"[5] although it is usual to consider many Spanish novels of the past fifteen years as neo-realistic. Normally the term concerns a specific novelistic technique, but what is understood in the case just cited is a "way of feeling the impetuous current of life in each instant. It is not a fashion . . . .Characters, problem and form must be of absolute fidelity to the present." While *Diary of a Hunter* lacks the degree of social criticism found in a majority of "neo-realistic" Spanish novels, it does fit some of the norms, particularly that of the novelist's removal of self as viewpoint, allowing the reader to judge, to conclude, and evaluate. In this respect the technique is "objective," even though Delibes did not pretend to have written an objectivist novel.

In *Diary of a Hunter*, as in *The Path*, formal plot has been all but totally suppressed in favor of the development of a character, central consciousness, or perspective, thus revealing to the reader a series of anecdotes, without a clear beginning or definitive end, simply a "slice of life" in a given time. The first *Diary* covers from the 15th of August to the 25th of January of the second year thereafter, about a year and a half, including two hunting seasons. At the beginning, Lorenzo is looking forward to the imminent reopening. The reader witnesses his suffering after that season's end, and sees his glee repeated when the new season opens. Near the end, he is already dreading the season's close in March. The *Diary* is definitely structured around Lorenzo's passion, as its title would indicate. However, there are also other relatively significant events in his life, close to the beginning and end of the *Diary*, so that it produces the sensation of having covered a more or less unified period, even though most of the incidents have no unity other than that conferred by the personality of the protagonist. The beginning and end, for example, are not interrelated, not equal to the traditional beginning and end of a plot, but do constitute breaks in the otherwise rather even tenor of Lorenzo's existence. On August 15th, the date of the first page of the *Diary*, he has just changed jobs, leaving the Institute, where he had been employed for some time, to take a post as beadle in the School of Commerce in Valladolid. Because of Delibes' association with this school, some believed *Diary of a Hunter* to be a *roman à clef*, a novel in which the characters had recognizable real-life counterparts. According to the novelist, certain people associated with the school were offended by what they considered to be personal allusions. This, however, was not his intention;

resemblances between characters and incidents in the novel and identifiable individuals are fortuitous and coincidental.

At the novel's close, Lorenzo's mother is paralyzed, on her deathbed, and he realizes for the first time how much he depended on her. There is a last-page reconciliation with his girlfriend, Anita, with whom he had broken after one of many quarrels over his time spent hunting. These events prepare the way for the second *Diary*, which begins after Lorenzo's mother has died, and he has married Anita. Both *Diaries* are made up of a series of anecodotes and semi-random incidents, unified by the protagonist, and lack a traditional plot. However, the second *Diary* has a greater coherence than the first, in that its individual episodes constitute one larger and clearly defined period in Lorenzo's life, his "American adventure," lasting approximately one year. Included in the events of the first *Diary* are many that are in themselves insignificant, and others of greater importance: the deaths of several characters ("el Mele," son of Lorenzo's best friend; Lorenzo's sister's baby; and a hunting friend); a number of births (a second "Mele," and his sister's twins); two weddings; the ups and down of Lorenzo's romance; and the progressive illness of his mother. These serve to give the flavor of life as an ongoing cycle, although many are given minor stress, relegated to the background. While Lorenzo's degree of involvement in such events varies, none is able to rouse in him the impassioned response that hunting evokes. Delibes has renounced much of the dramatic potential of these incidents, for Lorenzo often relates them in a cursory, offhand and low-keyed fashion, occasionally approaching the appearance of indifference. This caused some Spanish critics to see Lorenzo as a rather callous character, for in his *Diary* a birth, wedding, or funeral usually receives less attention than a dispute over matters of the hunt, or his jubilant recounting of a lucky shot. On the other hand, since for Delibes the major factor which would stimulate a character such as Lorenzo to keep a diary is his pride and passion as a hunter, such a slanted focus is necessary.

The novel is a prime example of naturalness and simplicity, well composed in spite of a surprising limitation of material and resources. This causes a deceptive impression of facility. The hunter-narrator is in no way an exceptional personality; there is nothing outstanding or singular about Lorenzo, his life, or even his hunting prowess. Nor does anything unusual or startling happen; the events are part of everyday life in any class or country. In fact, Lorenzo is the type who normally makes little or no impression upon others, yet despite a certain psychological ordinariness and commonplaceness, he amuses, captivates, and overflows with vitality. His life is humble, his preoccupations simple, his problems elementary, his aspirations prosaic, and his love life ingenuous, with all these things told in the unpretentious and popular speech of the man in the street, the conversational style of the nearly illiterate. Although Lorenzo works in a modest center of higher learning, he seems to suffer no contagion from the environment; he gives not the slightest hint of a desire for further instruction, nor does he evince concern with culture or problems of expression. (In the second *Diary,* in which the character of Lorenzo has evolved somewhat, he has picked up a few learned and semi-learned phrases.)

Lorenzo as conceived by Delibes is almost totally incapable of having a literary style or of worrying about language, despite the fact that Delibes subsequently saw language as such as the protagonist of these two works. Certainly, finding an adequate medium of expression for Lorenzo must have been one of the most difficult technical obstacles faced by Delibes, for it is not easy from the point of view of a narrator of not inconsiderable culture and awareness to create autobiographical fiction using as its basis an uncultured character of unreflecting and quite ordinary mentality. Perhaps this, as well as a probable reaction to certain negative criticisms of the first Lorenzo, accounts for his evolution in the sequel to a somewhat more thoughtful personality.

Lorenzo's work in the School of Commerce produces a very modest salary, covering only the most pressing necessities. He reluctantly seeks extra work for his free time, tending a boiler and ushering in a movie theater to supplement the insufficient income and to finance his "vice," hunting. Even with these measures, he must carefully count the bullets he can use on a given day, and plan ahead for months to purchase another gun. While Lorenzo is to some extent a victim of the Spanish economy, it must be confessed that he is not overly ambitious, despite his extra jobs, and these usually last only while the hunting season is closed. His friends are humble people, of similar socio-economic circumstances, mostly laborers and minor clerks. He belongs to a *tertulia*[6] of hunters, meeting in a café to play dominoes, discuss future hunting expeditions, or retell past venatic achievements. Once the season opens, the group meets less often, although its members see each other to organize excursions for weekends and holidays. Some of these companions, Tochano, Melecio, el Pepe, and Zacarías, appear with a certain frequency in the first *Diary.*

Usually connected with the hunting expeditions are slightly self-conscious descriptions of the Castilian landscape. While these are couched in a thoroughly credible language, popular and without literary pretensions, Lorenzo apparently feels that it is not entirely masculine to be too responsive to a beautiful morning or a rainy-day sunset. But nevertheless, he transmits to the reader his sensations of the high plain, the plowed fields, the cold and snows of December, a sudden wilderness storm, an August dawn. A parallel could be drawn between Lorenzo's attitude toward nature and religion, for while he is devout enough to go to mass before his predawn excursions, he suffers no metaphysical intranquility, no doubts, and of course no mystical tendencies.

The two *Diaries* are difficult reading, for many of the expressions used by Lorenzo are unfamiliar even to the native speaker of Spanish. His lexicon includes many localisms, sayings peculiar to the country people with whom he talks during hunting trips, slang and colloquialisms, a few vulgar and occasionally profane terms, popular proverbs and folk sayings, and of course the language peculiar to the hunt itself. Much of this will not be found in Spanish dictionaries, and upon occasion the local Castilian dialects vary so that villagers cannot always understand those from as close as fifteen miles away. This makes it extremely difficult to translate the *Diaries,* and the result would hardly be rewarding, as one of their great values would be mutilated, lost, or changed beyond recognition. Unfortunately, no rendering in another language can quite convey the flavor of Lorenzo's diction. The second *Diary,* if anything, is more difficult linguistically than the first, and some critics have considered it inferior to its predecessor because of the proliferation of colloquial "Americanisms."

Various typical characteristics of Delibes' narrative art are repeated in *Diary of a Hunter:* the use of nicknames, the repetition of certain phrases (Lorenzo is addicted to a limited number of favored expressions), and a tendency to caricature. This caricature does not seem to serve a primarily critical intent, but may be employed for the sake of humor, or may result as an almost inevitable consequence of the narrative perspective. Since all other characters are viewed through the eyes of Lorenzo, who could not be too astute psychologically, his simplified version of their acts and motivations naturally tends to produce caricature.

Lorenzo, like the parallel protagonists of "The Rails," has a motivation for material self-improvement, but like them, he has certain personal flaws which stand in the way of any significant advancement. Something of a dreamer and optimist, he is addicted to the lottery, and while not successful until the end of the second *Diary*, is able to keep his hopes alive. He is seen initially moving to a new home, over the objections of his mother, reluctant to leave the place she lived in for thirty years. Similarly, the sequel finds him leaving to start a new life in America, once more expecting to better his lot. This perpetually optimistic desire also recalls Sebastián, of *Still It Is Day*.

Lorenzo's passion for hunting has been at least partially inherited from his father; this is still another indication of how the possibilities inherent in determinism intrigue Delibes. Lorenzo's father, a fanatic hunter, had died some fifteen years previously, and three months after having lost his right hand in an accident. His death bewildered the doctors, but Lorenzo believes that he simply wasted away upon realizing he could no longer hold a gun, and the mother agrees that he died of sorrow. Lorenzo is convinced that if at any time age or some other cause prevents his hunting, he will die exactly as did his father.

The minute knowledge which Lorenzo displays of the habits of birds and other small game reflects Delibes' own intimate acquaintance with the countryside, its flora, and fauna. Like his creator, Lorenzo is seriously concerned with issues affecting the well-being of wildlife, particularly soil and forest conservation, the prosecution of poachers and enforcement of game laws, and the effective policing of such illicit practices as hunting at night with tractors and other machinery. Both Delibes and his protagonist are patriotically opposed to making of hunting a tourist attraction, something which happened in Spain in the past decade. They foresee the virtual extinction of certain species because of commercialization. While Lorenzo is enough of an instinctive hunter to shoot a rabbit before the season opens when one jumps up before him while he is out hunting birds, he does practice sufficient self-restraint to refuse to participate in large-scale marauding, and never intentionally plans ahead to shoot things out of season. He signs a petition supporting prosecution of game law violators. This act reflects a special concern of Delibes, who was active in having these laws strengthened and their enforcement tightened in Spain, although they apply only to the public domain, while the large preserves of private landowners are not policed. It is primarily in regard to this special privilege of wealth that the novel sounds its strongest note of social criticism, a protest entirely in character since it is part of the overall phenomenon of the hunt which most impassions Lorenzo.

Interspersed with accounts of his hunting adventures are incidents from Lorenzo's domestic life, visits from his sister Modes (perpetually broke, pregnant, and in tears), frequent disputes with the neighbors, and the necessity of saving the day when his mother absentmindedly let in the meter reader without removing a homemade device for cheating on the electric bill. There are numerous anecdotes connected with the School of Commerce: the romance and marriage of the teachers of French and German, the penniless professor for whom Lorenzo clandestinely sells copies of lectures, the ironically treated "investigation" when someone sketched a nude on a bulletin board. Lorenzo's relationship with Anita, his future wife, begins shortly after the opening pages, but even before their first date, the two quarrel over his hunting on Sundays. Both are stubborn, and while Lorenzo spends many tortured, sleepless nights, he is unable to renounce his other passion. After renewing their relationship, they quarrel almost immediately again, and this procedure is repeated several times during the next months. Lorenzo yields to the extent of returning early on Sunday evenings to take. Anita dancing. But their romance continues to be stormy, and while Lorenzo often mentions marriage, Anita refuses to commit herself.

Lorenzo wins a shooting match, which produces one of the longest entries in the *Diary,* revealing a certain ingenuous vanity, indirectly expressed. Shortly afterward, the periods between writing become longer and longer because of a more serious quarrel with Anita. One of the few events in these pages involves a case of mistaken identity: Lorenzo kills a shepherd's dog, believing it to be rabid, and subsequently lacks the courage to confess his error; this causes a series of nightmares. Another long section is devoted to a daydream, anticipating the second *Diary:* Lorenzo again hopes to win the lottery and imagines that with the quantity of wild game in America and his hunting ability, he could establish a canning factory there and become a millionaire. This ends the next day after learning he has not won; he feels poorer than before, having lost his dream. One political note is included, as the students demonstrate for the return of Gibraltar to Spain, and Lorenzo joins them. The overall effect of these and other anecdotes is to give the sensation of the ebb and flow of life from day to day, with enough repetition or interlocking of entries to allow the reader to feel that he knows what has happened in the day not covered. There is thus an impression of continuity, though the presentation is discontinuous. Delibes has achieved a strong integration of personality and atmosphere which conveys unity to the other material.

The first *Diary* continues to be one of Delibes' most popular works with the public and with critics, despite the fact that in this case, too, there were some few who found certain passages morally offensive (indicative rather of the regime's puritanical mentality than of the nature of the book). If a few found Lorenzo's language off-color, many respectable critics felt that this same colorfulness was the work's greatest single value or attraction. What is surprising, in view of the book's reception and the honors accorded it, is that apparently no serious linguistic study has been attempted, nor has it been the subject of any detailed analysis. There are numerous laudatory reviews and some slightly deprecating ones, but no penetrating critical investigations.

II Diario de un emigrante
(Diary of an Emigrant)[7]

This is the second of Lorenzo's diaries; it carries a brief prologue in which Delibes quotes a supposed popular saying to the effect that "second parts are never good," presumably based on a similar passage by Cervantes. Like Cervantes, Delibes also takes advantage of the time lapse between the two parts to use his opening pages to reply to criticism which has appeared in the meantime. He is particularly concerned with defending the verisimilitude of a diary's being written by a personality like Lorenzo, and anticipates further criticism of his having brought out a second installment. Delibes holds that the writer is not entirely autonomous, but occasionally finds he has not gotten some theme or character "out of his system" with one book, necessitating a second or a third or more.

The previous *Diary* had ended on January 25th, a Monday; the sequel begins on January 24th, also Monday. Although no year is given, it would seem therefore (barring leap year) to be one year after the close of *Diary of a Hunter,* a supposition borne out by a reference to Anita's age near the end of the second *Diary.* Lorenzo and Anita are now married and expecting a child, but their relationship continues to be plagued by disputes over the time he spends hunting. The reader familiar with the previous work is aware that in the interim Lorenzo's mother has died and that his marriage is rather recent, but almost no effort is made to supply details on other events for the intervening period.

At the outset of *Diary of an Emigrant,* steamship tickets are received from Anita's uncle in Chile. Embarcation is sheduled for March 15th, and the six weeks interim is filled with preparations for departure. The complications of obtaining the extensive documentation required, related in some detail, may either reflect Lorenzo's ingenuousness or constitute a light satire of the bureaucratic red tape faced by Spaniards wishing to go abroad. Perhaps to some extent the involved procedure was calculated to discourage emigration, for the mass exodus of Spaniards, especially the young, has been most problematic in the last two decades, and has been the theme of novels by a number of writers. Delibes is seriously concerned with the causes for this mass emigration, as well as the results for those remaining behind. Lorenzo, while initially filled with optimistic anticipation, does not burn his bridges, but takes an extended leave instead of quitting his job. Jubilantly he looks forward to arriving in Chile in time for the opening of the hunting season in the Southern Hemisphere, but begins to suffer nostalgia at the thought of parting from his friends, especially his companion of fifteen years, Melecio. Thus the preparation for his eventual return begins even before leaving Spain.

The language of the second *Diary* is even more difficult to follow. Not only is the narrative continued in the inimitable lexicon of Lorenzo, but even before departure his writing begins to be sprinkled with "Americanisms" and terms peculiar to Chile, as he inserts quotations from the letters of Anita's uncle, Egidio. Once in Santiago, this linguistic exoticism becomes progressively more evident. Undoubtedly such colloquial and slang elements abound most in the speech of the less cultured, which is the social group with which Lorenzo usually associates in Chile. His initial reaction to the new language patterns is by turns bemused and superior, but he soon begins to assimilate them. The abundance of such innovations in Lorenzo's vocabulary testifies to Delibes' powers of observation; presumably he made some sort of list at the time of his brief visit to Chile some three years before writing *Diary of an Emigrant.* Unfortunately, as most of the innovations consist of variants for given words which would be translated by only one term, there is no way to preserve the flavor of the work in another language.

The weeks preceding Lorenzo's departure are heavy with sentiment, in contrast to his rather undemonstrative nature as seen in *Diary of a Hunter.* Perhaps this represents Delibes' response to criticism of the first *Diary:* some critics spoke of Lorenzo's seeming callousness, his almost complete lack of response to certain transcendent events, and this may have wounded his creator. The previously cited Prologue to the *Complete Works* describes Lorenzo in a fashion implicitly denying his apparent indifference, and Delibes has definitely made him more reflective and more overtly sentimental in his second appearance. Lorenzo wishes to take leave personally of each and every one of his old hunting grounds. Also, he is particularly moved by the farewell party organized by his friends, and almost cries upon selling his bicycle. The numerous attacks of nostalgia and homesickness, beginning before arrival and multiplying when the new life does not meet their rosy expectations, also contribute to make a more introspective character of Lorenzo.

During the prolonged transatlantic crossing, Lorenzo and Anita enjoy life as tourists and spend nearly all his small savings. They are all but penniless upon reaching Santiago, and at the mercy of Uncle Egidio, who seems willing to exploit Lorenzo financially, employing him at an unusually low wage while "learning the business." The uncle is a fanatic on saving money, and immediately criticizes Lorenzo's "vice," hunting. Hunting in Chile also disillusions Lorenzo, partly because he scorns the "easy" game, less wily than that in Spain, partly because he realizes that his enjoyment had depended upon sharing the expeditions with old friends. He is likewise disappointed to learn how expensive shells are, and by midway through the *Diary* has stopped his excursions. This, combined with Anita's unconfessed disappointment and her mania for listening to radio broadcasts from Spain, contributes to a growing discontent with the new life, while the old looks better each day. Lorenzo is also extremely uncomfortable because of the aunt's aggressively amorous interest in him, and is upset by the persistent earthquakes. Before long, the only thing preventing return to Spain is lack of money and the unwillingness to admit failure, the more so as he has written some imaginative success stories to his friends back home. After a quarrel with Uncle Egidio, Lorenzo and his wife move to a boarding house, and he takes work as a hotel elevator operator. The phrase "There's no place like home" is repeated with increasing frequency.

Lorenzo and a friend decide to open a shoeshine parlor, and both borrow money. This responsibility terrifies Lorenzo, but he calculates they can pay and realize some profit. His son is born on the opening day, multiplying his responsibilities, and the business goes badly from the beginning. There is a reconciliation with Uncle Egidio, who wished to be the baby's godfather, and Lorenzo becomes still more reflective, often "thinking about life," with the stimulus of his fatherhood and the sudden death of a friend. Upon learning that a family supplement is now being paid to workers of his class in Spain, Lorenzo finally confesses to himself that he has no intention of remaining, that he is working largely to be able to return. Supervising the business and retaining his other job, he becomes ill, and there is a two weeks' lapse in the diary. After a month off from work, he begins to renew his contacts in Spain by letter. However, during this time, Anita builds up a good clientele as a hairdresser and begins to prosper, which humiliates Lorenzo. He is fired from his job at the hotel because of an episode with the pursuing aunt, and takes over the shoeshine business personally, beginning to drink heavily. Incensed when a former employee appears as a client, he decides to sell, and closes the shine parlor.

The experience of Christmas in the summer is too much for Lorenzo, and he finally suggests to Anita that they return. While she has begun to adjust and does not receive the idea enthusiastically, Lorenzo is strengthened in this resolve after having sold the business for a small profit and having won a minor prize in the lottery. He hesitates upon learning that his father-in-law has informed his friends at home that his letters were full of lies, but decides that the damage is done, and within a week has bought tickets to return. Most of their money is spent on presents, and although Lorenzo is surprised to feel a last-minute nostalgia upon leaving Chile, he begins the trip home filled with happy anticipation.

The decision to return is completely convincing, as the *Diary* is filled with frequent hints of its eventuality. Seen in retrospect, what is less convincing is Lorenzo's having left Spain in the first place. He is presented in the first *Diary* as interested in material advancement, particularly if it is easy, and presumably this is his motive. Many times during the approximately ten months in Chile, Lorenzo repents of his "greed," rationalizing that after all he was not so poor in Spain. Since the development of motivation for the emigration presumably belongs to the period that elapsed between the two *Diaries,* the reader is left feeling that the whole trip was the result of an impulse. Lorenzo is a great deal like his creator: he is not of the stuff of which emigrés are made.

CHAPTER 7

The Travel Books

DELIBES' four travel books do not purport to be tourist guides; they are simply records of personal impressions, reactions, and opinions, which he does not offer as superior to those of any other traveler. Because of their frequently subjective nature, they can be more revealing at times of their author's personality and ideas than his works of fiction. Delibes points out that there are various ways to see the world: "jumping from rock to rock, from sanctuary to sanctuary, or even from cabaret to cabaret."[1] To this he adds his own personal approach, neither better nor worse, but very definitely his own. As a traveler, Delibes attempts to avoid the preconceived or planned, the formal tour, in favor of more natural and spontaneous experiences. He rejects what he calls "fossilized" trips and the rigidity of timetables and fixed itineraries. It is his belief that the world should present "a new discovery for each and every pair of eyes," and to this end must be seen on a completely individual basis.

Delibes' viewpoint in this respect is surprisingly relativistic. He asserts that there are "as many worlds as there are years, and these are as varied as the pair of eyes which contemplate (them)."[2] This attitude is close to the perspectivism of Ortega y Gasset, as is Delibes' affirmation that "the world of yesterday is not that of today, nor does that which one (person) sees resemble in the slightest what is perceived by his neighbor."[3] It is in this conceptual framework that Delibes presents his travel books, not as a definitive view, but one individual perspective.

These works are written for the most part with few literary pretensions. Their style, if any, is largely journalistic, with some chapters originally composed as "chronicles" for newspapers in Spain, and later assembled for publication in volume form. Delibes is an alert observer, tending to concentrate on the concrete; however, at times his observations of specifics do lead him to conclusions about generalities, not always with fortunate results. Such general conclusions are usually in the vein of the obsessive thematics of his narratives and probably reveal a predisposition to interpret in a given fashion, or to look for certain things in each country. For example, he is led to conclude that one of the defining characteristics of our age is velocity, which he also calls lack of stability (in other words, mobility), "nomadism" both in daily life and tourism. There is a perceptible relationship between such an observation and his novelistic preoccupation with emigration and the city versus country theme.

Delibes' travel books are sincere, spontaneous and human, without any more transcendent pretension than to record his impressions of a given place and moment. Because of their simplicity, straight-forwardness, lack of concern with style, and subjective impressionism, the author as human being is more accessible, more intimately revealed, than in his writings with more transcendent concerns. As the travel books also contain political reflections and social ideas mixed in among impressions of the journey, those seeking ample acquaintance with Delibes the man will find their perusal rewarding. What these accounts do not offer are descriptions of monuments, museums, and the usual "sights," for with the exception of a few landscapes, Delibes prefers to concentrate on the human element, the daily life, the economy, and varying national characters.

I   Por esos mundos (Round About the World)

The first part of this volume appeared originally as a separate work entitled *Un novelista descubre América (A Novelist Discovers América)*,[4] including impressions of Brazil, Argentina, and Chile. Some five years later, a new edition incorporated pages on the Canary Islands, and the title was changed to *Por esos mundos*. Actually there is little unity between these parts, aside from their sharing the same narrative veiwpoint, the same observer; however, in the introductory lines preceding his pages on the Canaries, Delibes justifies combining the two with the idea that it is in these islands that Europe and America meet. He finds in the islanders characteristics of both Spaniards and Latin Americans, and feels there is a logical link.

Delibes suggests in preliminary words before the first section that, had he reelaborated his impressions afterward, he might have produced a longer, more impressive work, filled with more profound reflections and profuse documentation, but he has not done so in the belief that it would falsify his real experience. In travel, he affirms, there is nothing like the first impression, nothing more valuable than the initial reaction of the "virgin" consciousness. He uses as a point of departure the premise that one who is too wordly cannot profit from travel; to benefit, one must have an unjaded perception, a clear and perhaps slightly naive awareness. Only the eyes and consciousness of a rustic, he suggests, can receive the full impact. Obviously, this explains a good deal about the artistic gestation of *Diary of an Emigrant*. At the time that Delibes made his first visit to Buenos Aires, the flight lasted some forty hours, the prolonged time aloft making even more overwhelming his first glimpse of the gigantic spectacle of Brazil. Some of his most lyric pages are devoted to its natural panorama, its luxurious vegetation, its immensity. One of his strongest initial impressions of America is of hugeness, enormous extension in size and space. He was likewise overwhelmed by the sprawling expanse of Buenos Aires and its monumental airport, although this did not prevent his reflecting that the latter is "one of those excesses behind which dictators conceal their mediocrity."[5] Accustomed, however, to the smaller scale of Spanish towns and cities, their arrangement in self-contained neighborhoods, and the relative scarcity of automobiles, Delibes concludes that so huge a metropolis would be most uncomfortable as a permanent residence. He criticizes the public transportation system, the trains, and taxis, but despite finding the distances inconvenient, considers Argentina a country of opportunity and of the future. Another particularly vivid impression is the result of a thirty-eight hour train ride across Argentina; Delibes was especially affected by the expanse of the pampas, and the great herds of cattle.

One chapter is devoted to "the gigantic spectacle of the Andes," and another to the Chilean paradise for hunters and fishermen, two attractions with great appeal for Delibes. The reader will find numerous parallels between these chapters and the reactions of Lorenzo in *Diary of an Emigrant*, with other anticipations of his experience in the sections on the Chilean character and the local diet (not to the taste of Delibes or his fictional creation). Also like Lorenzo, Delibes experienced without pleasure the almost-daily earthquakes, and focuses for a time on this phenomenon and its causes. The picturesque figure of the *roto*, a lower extreme of Chilean society, also receives particular scrutiny, foreshadowing the appearance of several *rotos* in the second *Diary*.

In one of the most moving passages in his travel works, Delibes describes a visit to the southern tip of Chile, with particular emphasis on the pathetic spectacle of the Arauco Indians. This tribe, once such noble warriors that their bravery inspired a conquering Spanish captain to celebrate the prowess in epic poetry,[6] has today been reduced by the Spanish imposition of "civilization" to a handful of enervated and apathetic alcoholics. With sorrow and shame, the novelist contemplates the physical and mental degeneracy that white domination has produced, the indifference, near-immobility, and loss of will to live.

The pages on the Canaries deal mainly with the island of Tenerife and its capital, with particular notice of the climate and el Teide, Tenerife's great volcano, the highest peak in Spain. In addition to the geography, Delibes is attracted by the psychology of the islanders, for him something between the Andalusian and Chilean. He is also interested in the island's economy. There are tourism, agriculture (particularly bananas), and the harbor of Santa Cruz, an important port of call for transatlantic ships. The attention devoted to these factors reflects the novelist's commercial training, and the repeated emphasis on varying local character, his constant interest in man.

II   Europa, parada y fonda (Europe, Stops and Inns)[7]

The second of Delibes' travel books collects impressions of his travels at various times in four countries: Italy (1956), Portugal (1957), Germany (1960), and France (visited more than once but included primarily as seen en route to Italy). The author states that this "is not a political book, nor has it any philosophical pretentions. It is simply a small, impartial and rather frivolous volume of human impressions, collected along the roadways" (p. 12). Although Delibes denies any transcendent intent, the book does contain reflections on such things as the shift in the relative positions of the nations of the world, depriving Europe of its traditional hegemony. Alleging that he is insufficiently endowed to develop this theme, however, Delibes renounces it after a few pages.

Traveling to Italy from Spain by automobile, the novelist records his impressions of towns along the Azure Coast, the French and Italian Rivieras, paying special attention once more to national differences. He compares the laconic French with the gesticulating, effervescent Italians, and while he does not state his preference, it seems to be inclined toward the latter. Delibes' commercial background comes to the fore in a chapter entitled "Miracle in Milan," expressing admiration for the postwar reconstruction, industrialization, and well-organized traffic patterns. On the other hand, he was rather negatively affected by Venice, calling the gondola a "third-class coffin." The absence of cars and the relative quiet, combined with his disappointment in the city's legendary coloring and an atmosphere he found funereal, produced for Delibes a macabre sensation, making the black gondola sinister and lugubrious, a feeling intensified when he learned that the same vessels also serve as hearses. While admitting the gondola's appropriateness for the physiognomy of the city, Delibes was far from experiencing the usual tourist's romantic thrill.

His remarks on Italy tend to be dominated by the themes of industry, new highways, and traffic problems, but include some sections with political overtones. Florence he found overcrowded, as his visit coincided with the climax of political campaigning. Delibes considered the oratory quite out of keeping with the city's beauty and traditions, but was favorably impressed with the political sophistication of those he met, as partly alignments seemed to present no obstacle to cordial coexistence. Although he believed the Italians to be generally rather skeptical in political matters, he expresses his admiration for the achievements of the Christian Democrats, particularly for Gronchi and his work for the cause of the proletariat. Probably mindful of the situation in Spain, Delibes reiterates his political ignorance and insists on the purely subjective character of his observations. The novelist is not one to be overly influenced by accepted opinions, and thus was favorably impressed by the inhabitants of Naples, despite their vicious reputation.

In his visit to Portugal, Delibes was initially surprised by the excessive architectural adornment, later postulating the theory that this tendency is the result of a national timidity and desire to hide one's handiwork. Most of his reactions to the Portuguese are favorable, and he mentions in particular the traits of discretion, timidity, politeness, hospitality, obsequiousness, and relative quiet (compared with Spaniards) as outstanding national characteristics. For Delibes, disliking the hustle and bustle of mechanized civilization, Portugal's relatively untraveled roads were a pleasure, although he scrutinized the standards of living and noted some things needing improvement. He contrasts the apparent fertility of the soil with the evident poverty of the peasants, and remarks on the concentration of wealth in a few families, while stipulating that the level of life in Portugal is not so bad as he had been led to expect. The fact that the novelist was impressed by the volume of imports in Lisbon is a direct reflection of the scarcities in Spain at the corresponding time. Delibes' principal disappointment in Portugal was the Shrine of Fatima, overcommercialized from his viewpoint and lacking in taste, particularly as nothing had been done to preserve the natural environment. He found more religious sentiment in the surrounding countryside than in the shrine itself.

Delibes traveled to Germany in the winter, via Switzerland, and greatly admired the level Swiss roads through the mountains, the good sense, methodical organization, and hard work he perceived as national characteristics, but for him the Swiss personality seemed overly cold, frigid, and geometrical. He writes at some length on the reconstruction of Germany in postwar years, unreservedly praising the German psychology, quite unlike the Spanish, with serious timetables, the gift of organization, and persistence. Given Delibes' professional training, he was particularly interested by the German economy, manifested in the number of automobiles, rapidity and facility of travel, architectural innovations and mechanization. The tour of the former concentration camp and extermination center at Dachau moved and horrified him, and he includes a description as a warning for the future. Delibes encountered many Spaniards working in Germany, and following his interest in the problems of emigration, spoke with many, and records especially their homesickness for Spain.

III USA y yo (USA and I)[8]

Perhaps those pages of Delibes devoted to this country are among his most revealing for Americans. The author remarks in his prologue that one reader of the manuscript commented that it disclosed more about Delibes than about the United States. Another suggested that the shock produced by the impact between a rural Castilian and the most advanced nation in the world was, to say the least, amusing. Delibes explains that the title is due not to any lack of modesty on his part, but to a wish to emphasize the volume's personal and subjective nature. "I do not dare to say that the United States are thus and so, but only that thus I have seen them" (p. 9).

Delibes was frankly overwhelmed, beginning with his first glimpse, by the immensity of the "megalopolis," the gigantic buildings of New York, the enormous industrial complexes of the metropolitan area and the expanse southward, seen as he was driven to Washington. While admiring the obvious general prosperity and vigor of the economy, he felt vaguely threatened, sensing much destructive potential. For him, the tremendous proportions and the automation menace the individual; man could be swallowed by his own inventions. Delibes was depressed to find so little remaining in this area of "God's handiwork," yet simultaneously awed by the proportions of American technology. Certain things that the average American takes for granted awoke his enthusiasm, such as the steel bridges which Delibes compared to Gothic cathedrals. His reactions are an ambivalent mixture of marvel at the material abundance, and an entirely predictable dislike of certain extremes of mechanization. Half-jokingly, but in a fashion revealing his amazement, the novelist comments that one of the quickest indexes of the differences between the American and European economies is the garbage heaps, especially automobile graveyards.

As in his other travels, Delibes is especially interested in the observation of national psychological differences. He finds Americans a people with comparatively few social, professional, or aristocratic prejudices, and comments on the absence of the *machismo* (exaggerated masculinity) complex in American males. Practicality, pragmatism, discipline, haste, industriousness, and punctuality are among the qualities cited as distinctive. He finds Americans as a whole to be strong, but awkward physically, and lacking the Mediterranean effusiveness. Delibes comments frequently upon the extensive use of the automobile, the infrequent utilization of legs and feet, and theorizes that this may have something to do with the awkwardness.

One chapter is devoted to protest in America, although based almost exclusively on its manifestations in Greenwich Village. Accustomed to the European standard of apartment residence, Delibes was intrigued by American one-family dwellings, porches and yards, and the care given thereto. Although he considered Americans cordial and endowed with various civic virtues, they are at the same time relatively cold, undemonstrative by comparison with Latins, correct but rather indifferent, tolerant and not overly inquisitive, but likewise not too interested in the problems of others. These traits, together with what he qualifies as a certain isolationist tendency in the individual may be, Delibes speculates, the result of mechanization, of each person's solitude as proferred by his own automobile, the preponderance of one-family dwellings, and the general lack of servants. The emancipation of women, American marriage and divorce also receive his scrutiny, as does the family institution. Delibes concludes, critically, that this is a society with no place for the aged.

American cooking and kitchens, the special and characteristic American fears or phobias, the treatment of children, education,

universities, confidence in the individual, religion, the Mormons and
Amish, various social problems, liberty, elections, racial integration,
poverty, and agricultural prosperity are among the topics examined by
Delibes in a book which comes as close to memoirs as to an orthodox
travel volume. It must be remembered, of course, that his experience
was not simply tourism, as he lived for a year in the United States,
allowing for more detailed social observation. One chapter is given to
death, not surprising considering the importance of this theme in his
other works. The American handling of death, like many other matters,
is seen to have both positive and negative aspects: while the novelist
approves the de-emphasis of lugubriousness and theatricality, he finds
the funerals overcommercialized or often lacking in dignity.

Delibes' impressions of the United States are limited to the East
Coast and part of the Midwest, with emphasis on New York and
Washington, D.C. A majority of his descriptions involve intangibles of
social phenomena that not every traveler would observe. Despite the
fact that *USA and I* is provided with a good number of photographs,
unlike his other travel books, few of these represent the usual tourist
"sights." More often they illustrate the economy, education or daily
life, the things which most interested Delibes.

IV La primavera de Praga (Springtime in Prague)[9]

In this fourth and final volume to date recording the novelist's
travels, the tendency noted in earlier such works is increased so as
virtually to exclude the content of the travel guide or tourist handbook.
Attention is concentrated almost entirely upon the people, the
economy, and the political situation; geographical notes are few and far
between, and the city is described only briefly in the final half-dozen
pages. While Delibes, with customary frankness, emphasized the
subjective and even emotional nature of his response to the events and
circumstances viewed, this visit was one of his shortest, some two
weeks, and the resulting generalizations must be considered more
impressionistic and less authoritative than would be true if based on
lengthier experience. Here, too, the language barrier was greater.

In *Springtime in Prague* Delibes exposes more clearly than in any
book to date his social idealism. Enthused after witnessing firsthand the
short-lived experiment at democracy within socialism, he nonetheless
mused that the world has not achieved the maturity to "accept the
fundamental conquests of socialism as an integral part of inalienable

human rights" (p.13). Among these, he lists absolute equality in education, participation by all the people in political administration, suppression of oligarchies, agrarian reform, equitable distribution of income, and the right—and obligation—to work. Each man's self-realization to the extent of his capacities, believes Delibes, does not require the suppression of political rights or the prohibition of private initiative. It seems to be his feeling that the mechanisms of tyranny characterizing the Socialist revolution are necessities imposed by human "immaturity," egotism, and the unwillingness to accept freely these humanitarian and Christian principles.

While Delibes reiterates his lack of political experience, his ignorance, and inadequate sociological and economic preparation for treating the subject, the primary purpose of *Springtime in Prague* is to describe the Czechoslovakian effort to achieve liberty and democracy within communism. In this connection, Delibes insists upon his amateur status, but at the same time is openly admiring of the progress achieved during the short-lived but significant "Springtime in Prague." The title has a double meaning, referring not only to the time of Delibes' visit, but the Czech name for their political "thaw." Much of the book is in the form of a dialogue betwen the traveler and an unidentified but rather obtuse, bourgeois interlocutor, who is interested only in the material progress of the Czechs and not in the political, religious, or economic concessions of the regime. Thus Delibes is able implicitly to attack the position of Spanish capitalism without directing a word against it, effectively showing the narrow-mindedness and selfishness of the mentality presented.

Delibes examines with special interest the students, the economy, state enterprises, tips, the standard of living, highways, and markets, much as in earlier travel accounts. However, the abstract content is much greater, as several sections deal with ideological problems, religion, education, and political life. Personal notes include a semi-humorous, semi-Kafkaesque incident involving the extraction of a tooth, and a few words on local hunting. Continuing interests previously cited, Delibes reflects upon the family and divorce in Czechoslovakia, the position of women, and the national attitude toward death. Only brief mention is given the landscape and a few monuments in Prague.

Travel books have undergone a considerable resurgence of popularity in postwar Spain, cultivated by many writers of Delibes' generation who have found this ostensibly innocuous and even frivolous genre a convenient point of departure for any number of dissertations-in-disguise on social and political matters. In the tradition of the eighteenth-century precedent set by Cadalso's *Cartas marruecas,* many of Delibes' observations imply a satiric reflection upon corresponding situations in Spain, and his travel works can only be fully understood and appreciated by keeping them in constant mental comparison with the Spanish circumstances. Despite the long tradition of cultivation of travel literature by important writers, and despite the considerable biographical, ideological, and artistic significance of many such works, there is almost no secondary material describing the volume of travel books produced in postwar Spain. Delibes' travel works have likewise gone virtually unnoticed by the critics.

CHAPTER 8

The Theme of Aging

VARIOUS of Delibes' works give indications of his interest in old age and its problems. There may be some connection between this preoccupation and his childhood recollection of his father as "always old, always white-haired." And the relevance of the theme of aging to the novelist's obsessive concern for death is obvious. The first treatment of extreme age in a novel of Delibes occurs in *Still It Is Day*. The grandmother of Aurora (fiancée of the protagonist) figures in several scenes, among the most naturalistic in Delibes' production. The old woman is an almost loathsome picture of senility, an unfortunate but repugnant example of mental and physical deterioration. Near-blind, near-deaf, and near idiocy, she is a toothless, drooling mass of rumbling intestines. A quite different example of aging is "Nilo el viejo" in "The Walnut Trees." This old man is past eighty and still nimble enough to climb trees, still active and alert. Living in close contact with nature, he resembles another vigorous old peasant, the interlocutor of the author in *Hunting the Red Partridge*.

Further concern for the aged is evinced briefly in one of Delibes' travel books, *USA and I,* in which he voices the criticism that American society seems to have no place for the elderly, those who have ceased to be active. The hunter-priest in *Diary of a Hunter* occupies a midpoint between the extremes of physical decadence and a hale and hearty old age. He continued to pursue his avocation so long as his health permitted, and when too afflicted by rheumatism for further sallies, still carried on many ecclesiastical functions. "El centenario," the one-hundred-year-old villager in *The Rats* is, not surprisingly, also repugnant physically, the more so as a cancer has devoured half his face. Nevertheless, this old man's mind is clear, and he is an important source of knowledge for the child protagonist.

As suggested above, this theme is closely linked to Delibes' preoccupation with death, and in some of the cases just cited, the aged characters do in fact die. Nowhere in the novelist's work, however, are the two themes more dramatically linked than in *La hoja roja (The Red Leaf)*.[1] This novel constitutes Delibes' most extensive and intensive examination of aging and related phenomena, and is filled from beginning to end by the menacing shadow of death (more than once identified by the author as the true protagonist). Death is the obsession of Don Eloy, the ostensible protagonist and one of the two important figures. Perhaps it would be more correct to qualify death as the antagonist. There are other factors in Don Eloy's difficulties, but all are in some way related to age, while many of his picturesque or pathetic eccentricities are traceable to his fear of dying.

I   La hoja roja (The Red Leaf)[2]

While much of the novel consists of retrospection and memories, the first event in its presentation is the banquet celebrating the retirement of Don Eloy as a municipal functionary after fifty-three years of service. The scene resembles that described in the short story, "El traslado" ("The Transfer"), as both guests of honor, unaccustomed to the luxury, eat and drink too much and behave awkwardly and somewhat foolishly. The general boredom, impatience, or indifference of those gathered supposedly to honor them also is present in the two stories. But the situation in *The Red Leaf* is much more skillfully handled, and the old man succeeds in making his speech—monotonous, interminable, and repetitive. Don Eloy has probably never been an original thinker, but the many years in the same job have so molded his mentality that everything is related to the municipality. One of his overpowering interests seems to have been the efficient functioning of the garbage and sanitation service, and during many years this constituted a principal topic of conversation for him, as well as a major irritant for his wife.

While most people would experience some difficulty in adjusting to retirement after more than half a century at the same position, this is only part of Don Eloy's problem. He is tortured by a former friend's remark, some twenty years earlier, that "retirement is the waiting room of death." Once relegated to his unwelcome leisure, he has little to do but to turn this idea over endlessly in his mind. His wife (never close) has died; his one surviving son has long since left for a better life in Madrid, and Don Eloy has reached an age which offers few natural breaks in the monotony of existence other than the occasional deaths of contemporaries and old friends. His pension is too small to allow him to indulge his one hobby, photography, and Don Eloy eventually realizes that he is not welcome as a spectator in the photo clubs and supply stores.

Don Eloy's entire life has been insignificant; he has believed himself to be a center of attention on only three occasions: his wedding, a long-ago disastrous public appearance at the Photographic Society, and the night of his retirement. Actually, with Delibes' presentation of this third situation and reminiscences of the second, it seems clear that Don Eloy always repelled attention more than he attracted it. His marriage was far from happy, and if he was not miserable, it was because he asked so little; actually, neither his wife nor surviving son had any fondness for him. Don Eloy's problematic situation thus results not merely from advanced age and retirement, although these make his solitude and difficulties more acute. His income drops, but severe economic limitations offer no challenge in his circumstances, only imposing further restrictions on the possible solutions for Don Eloy's boredom and restlessness, reducing the chances of escape from loneliness.

The theme is not a common one in Spanish literature, although a superficially similar situation is treated by the great nineteenth-century novelist, Pérez Galdós, in *Miau*. The area of coincidence is the presentation of the financial difficulties of the bureaucrat who finds himself "retired," whether because of a change in political adminis-tration, for age, or other reasons. But Galdós' protagonist is not a lonely, provincial old man, and the two works are developed quite differently. While neither protagonist has a happy home life, and both figures combine varying degrees of the grotesque and the pathetic, the intent of the writers diverges after consideration of the problems of the government functionary out of work. In the case of *Miau,* the primary purpose is to satirize the false appearances under which this class lived, attempting to seem wealthy by borrowing heavily. Only incidentally does the protagonist seem to be the victim of the political spoils system. In *The Red Leaf* no change of administration is involved, but Don Eloy is a victim in a more subtle and terrible sense, for he has been used for fifty-three years, and then cast aside and forgotten, as Delibes makes clear in the ceremony "honoring" him, and the treatment he subsequently receives when he returns to visit his old office.

In *The Red Leaf* the novelist employs even more extensively his characteristic technique of repetition. Both Don Eloy and Desi, the

uneducated, elemental village girl who serves as his cook and
housekeeper, are given to repeating a few stories over and over. The old
man retrospectively idealizes a small number of childhood and youthful
memories and his dead son, and these anecdotes, despite frequent
retelling, fascinate the simple-minded maid. She in turn recalls again
and again incidents of life in her village, thereby combatting her
loneliness and homesickness. Repetition is also found in the introspective passages revealing the thoughts of Don Eloy, whose memory
returns obsessively to certain events, certain fears. The lengthy
repetitions serve also to emphasize the limited, closed-in or trapped
situations of the two protagonists, effectively underlining the essential
simplicity or primitiveness of their mentalities. But a certain lyric
pathos is achieved at times, as repetition and selection become in
Delibes' hands a powerful artistic device, permitting the reader to live
the atmosphere described.

Caricature also occurs in *The Red Leaf,* perhaps as a defense against
sentimentality or pathos, for the subject could easily lead to a more
somber or tearful treatment. However, the novelist seems to have been
aware of this danger, and constantly vigilant, managed to strike the
right balance between the ludicrous and pathetic, while avoiding the
extremes of both. The use of caricature permits a certain distance
between writer and subject, facilitating the attainment of this
equilibrium. Caricature is found, however, only in minor characters and
in only a few scenes involving the major figures; neither protagonist is
simply a caricature. Both have caricaturesque traits, and with a
different handling might indeed have been nothing more than exaggerated caricatures, but their psychologies are developed in a depth which
takes them beyond the superficial and parodic.

As in *The Path* and the two *Diaries,* the plot structure is loose, rather
imprecise, and open-ended, with little action of any importance.
Delibes prefers to emphasize presentation and description of character
and of situation. Significant events are few after Don Eloy's retirement,
not simply because of the novelist's interest in aspects other than
action, but because its lack makes even more powerful the monotony
and oppressiveness of the situation. Much of the novel unfolds Don
Eloy's slow realization that he has, in effect, simply ceased to exist
where practically everyone else is concerned. Don Eloy is a practicing
Catholic, but his dread of death is sufficient in itself to consititute a
motive for survival. He develops a number of hypochondriacal manias,
such as spending half an hour on his knees after eating to aid his

digestion, or negotiating the stairway bent over in a right angle to keep certain organs closer to the center of gravity. His life becomes a frantic struggle to prolong his existence on the one hand, and to escape from solitude on the other.

In organizing his novels for the *Complete Works* edition, Delibes included *The Red Leaf* in Volume Three[3] together with *Still It Is Day* and *The Rats,* a grouping characterized, he wrote, by "the preoccupation of the Other." This indicates clearly, considering these two last-named novels, that Delibes sees the situation of Don Eloy and others like him as a definite and pressing social problem and a resulting injustice that is neither religiously nor ethically justifiable. While Don Eloy has not lost his job to a machine, it would seem that for Delibes the mentality which sacrifices the individual to increased efficiency and speed is the real problem, regardless of the substitute. The novelist states in the Prologue to the volume just cited that "machines warm the stomach but chill the heart,"[4] and develops his notion that the rise in the standard of living in modern times has somehow produced an acute alienation of man from man. "Frivolity and haste do not let us see the individual" (p. 10), and despite the improved means of communication, men are paradoxically each day more alone. Solitude is identified by Delibes as one of the linking themes of these three novels, as each protagonist is radically alone, although the solitudes of Don Eloy and Desi "converge." When the secondary characters relate to the protagonists, observes the novelist, "they are not seeking them (the Other), but themselves." Delibes quotes Camus, "Men no longer know how to love," and affirms that this is pathetically, chillingly true. "The lack of love, the indifference for the Other—for the afflicted, the aged, the abnormal, the poor—is patent. And before such a phenomenon, general and progressive in all societies regardless of their organization, one comes to prefer hate to solitude, since at least feeling hated is to feel oneself accompanied."[5] These words situate *The Red Leaf* in the overall thought of Delibes, raising the problem above a merely local or political one to a more universal plane, even though the concrete dimension continues to exist.

The Red Leaf has not been too successful with the public, nor was it distinguished, once completed, by the awards and recognition received by some of Delibes' other works. In general, the criticism has been sparse, considering the importance of the novel, with no profound or lengthy studies. The relatively few critics devoting attention to *The Red Leaf,* however, have been near unanimous in their praise, and one called

Don Eloy and Desi "two of the best types of this literary century."[6]
The distinguished academician and critic, the late Melchor Fernández
Almagro, evoked the names of Quevedo and Goya when speaking of the
caricature employed in *The Red Leaf,* that of Valle-Inclán in relation to
the grotesque deformation of certain elements, and novelists such as
Galdós, "Clarín," and Cervantes when referring to the psychological
treatment of personalities which, despite caricature and symbolism, do
not lose human warmth and reality. He considers Don Eloy "the
firmest, most profoundly studied character of all his (Delibes')works."[7]

As did the two critics just cited, Rafael Vázquez Zamora feels that
Delibes represents the best Spanish novelistic tradition, with little or no
influence from current foreign or native literary fashions and fads. It is
his belief that Delibes prefers the elemental character to the intellectual
or complex personage precisely in order to "show the complexity of
the elemental beings which surround us." He attributes to Don Eloy
"an undeniable greatness," and affirms that he is "the most alive of all
the men created by Delibes, and this is precisely because he is waiting
to die, because his moribund vitality is concentrated in that futile
struggle of certain wild creatures mortally wounded. . . . The intensity
with which this grey, insignificant man, almost invisible for others, is
conscious of his old age, makes him tragically meaningful and
transcendental."[8] Vázquez Zamora points out the difficulties inherent
in the relationship of Don Eloy and Desi for the narrator, and indicates
that Delibes has skirted them with refinement and humor. For this
critic, *The Red Leaf* is "the most ironic and amusing—despite its
extremely sad essence—of the novels written by Delibes."

While there were some conservative elements in Spain (typified by
M. M. Astrián, critic of Radio Zaragoza) who found *The Red Leaf*
"vulgar and decadent," with a "crude theme," morally ambiguous
situations, and "vicious, brazen, Naturalistic language," such reactions
must be considered to be the result of political or ideological
disagreement with Delibes' message rather than a serious literary
analysis of the novel's content. It contains nothing offensive to
intelligent good taste. A review by a priest who is also a novelist, which
concentrated on moral and religious aspects, found nothing objection-
able, and had only praise for "the soft Christian light in which the
characters are presented," as well as the portrayal of the elementary
faith of Castile, represented by Desi. While he does not consider Delibes
a religious novelist, Father Martín Descalzo states his belief that
Delibes is well endowed to study, from the sociological viewpoint, the
religiosity of Castile, particularly its rural sectors.[9]

Antonio Vilanova indicates the relationship between *The Red Leaf* and the tradition of rural or regional *costumbrismo,* praising Delibes' acute powers of observation, the tenderness and warmth with which he treats a vulgar reality or absolutely ordinary, insignificant characters. For Vilanova, however, there is no deformation, satire, or caricature, but simply an extremely realistic vision of everyday contemporary life, the emotion and pathos hidden within the tragically ordinary personality. Despite its atmosphere of "desolation," he qualifies *The Red Leaf* as "an extremely beautiful novel," the "epic of domestic vulgarity imbued with the purest human values," a masterpiece of authenticity, emotion, and beauty.[10]

Paralleling the development of Don Eloy and his situation is the story of Desi, an illiterate, unattractive twenty-year-old who has left home to work, primarily because of need, but also because of her stepmother. Desi's moral and religious concepts are elementary, consisting largely of a great faith in the Virgin and in the efficacy of the one prayer she knows, the equivalent of "Now I lay me down to sleep." While she faithfully attends Mass, she is distracted even in the most solemn moments and prone to whisper to her companion. The anecdotes which Desi relates of her village are sufficiently numerous to give this novel a character both urban and rural, although the language is more in the vein of the rural novels and the two *Diaries.* Filling his unwanted leisure, but also for humanitarian reasons, Don Eloy undertakes to teach Desi to read, a section filled with delightful, subtle humor, as nearly all the practice texts come from the newspapers which apparently contain nothing but articles on Franco. Desi is slow, taking a year and five months simply to master the alphabet, but Don Eloy has plenty of free time.

Desi is a person with few illusions, but she has one dream, to marry Picaza, a rough, stuttering, bowlegged, ill-tempered boy from her village. Her hopes soar when he comes to the same city (presumably Valladolid) for his military service and begins to see her with some frequency. In a memorable scene on Christmas Eve, Don Eloy and Desi, both alone, decide to celebrate, and drink too much wine, singing until the neighbors protest. Marce, a friend of Desi, who works in the same building, tells Picaza with the idea that a little jealousy is a good thing, but apparently only succeeds in making him doubt Desi's virtue. Shortly after, when Don Eloy is out, he asks her to show him the apartment and attempts to rape her. Desi manages with great difficulty to fight him off, saying she never wishes to see him again, but mentally forgives him the same night. As Desi was providing him free laundry service, Picaza returns and resumes the relationship. When he finally mentions marriage, it is apparently only with the hope of facilitating seduction, but Desi lives for a time in ecstasy.

During this period, Don Eloy is crushed by the death of Don Isaías, his last surviving friend, and after days of brooding despondency, undertakes a trip to Madrid in hope of finding some human warmth and affection in his son. Thanks to the old man's sacrifices, León now has a prosperous legal career, has married a frivolous socialite, and wishes only to forget his obscure beginnings, including, of course, his father. Don Eloy's stay in León's house is extremely uncomfortable, and his daughter-in-law's treatment is a masterpiece of refined cruelty, while his son is openly hostile. He prolongs his stay, desperately hoping to wring some sign of affection from them, but finally admits defeat. He begins to think of his provincial apartment as a paradise by comparison, and in his mind Desi becomes almost angelically sweet. Returning, he finds Desi in tears, desolate because of her personal tragedy: Picaza is in prison, having killed a prostitute in a brawl.

Don Eloy comforts Desi and later takes her to a movie to distract her. Her ingenuous enjoyment is so great that he suggests skimping on the food budget in order to see movies more often, and their going out together becomes a habit. One of Don Eloy's manias is the cold, symbolic both of his fear of death and need for human warmth, and thus the arrival of spring is particularly significant. Don Eloy suggests that they celebrate, as at Christmas, with a bottle of wine and a meal together in the kitchen. Again Don Eloy drinks too much, and talks rather incoherently about the importance of warmth. He seizes Desi by the arm and begs her not to abandon him, suggesting they share the little he has, and when he dies, all will be hers. It is not entirely clear whether this is a proposal of marriage or simply a proposition, but Desi agrees with the same submissive words with which she customarily receives his orders. There is nothing romantic or even too optimistic about this ending, although Don Eloy has thereby escaped from solitude for his declining days, and Desi is able to submerge her own tragedy in the companionship of someone who needs her.

The title, "The Red Leaf," is repeated almost to the point of exasperation by Don Eloy, as he loses no occasion to use the one original metaphor coined in his lifetime. In the little books or packets of cigarette papers sold in Spain for those who roll their own, a red leaf appears to indicate there are only five remaining. Don Eloy applies this to his life: retirement is the "red leaf," and thus he has only five more.

He is seventy, and comes to take his metaphor seriously enough to believe that he has five years left to live, and for a time devotes most of his waking moments to mathematical calculations of how many days, hours, minutes, and seconds now remain.

There are certain changes in each of the protagonists before the end of the book which help to prepare the reader for a decisive moment in lives which have been largely tedium and routine. Don Eloy seems to undergo a reduction of his fear and obsession with death, although his quirks, tics, and manias continue. Desi overcomes her terror of the dark, and her subservience to Marce, acquiring an increased maturity and autonomy. This makes the joining of their fates a bit less desperate, more a matter of conscious choice. *The Red Leaf* is far from being a novel of simple entertainment, even though it contains passages among the most entertaining that Delibes has written. It is a novel subtly calculated to arouse feelings of guilt and responsibility, and this may explain its limited acceptance by the public. Commercial success, however, is often a poor index of the lasting worth of a work of literature, and many classics passed almost unnoticed in their times. *The Red Leaf* may well be such a work.

CHAPTER 9

On Hunting. Miscellaneous Works

DELIBES' two books on hunting and the collection of essays and articles bear somewhat the same relation to his overall production as do the travel books, insofar as they reveal things about the author which are less explicit in his fiction. Although his narratives are at times highly personal, they are less direct, and subject to imaginative deformation. The works considered here, with the exception of parts of *Viejas historias de Castilla la Vieja (Old Tales of Old Castile),* are almost totally nonfictitious and nonliterary. This does not mean that they are not thoroughly acceptable and occasionally admirable prose, but there are few artistic pretentions, little conventional structure, and seldom any emphasis on rhetorical aspects.

I La caza de la perdiz roja (Hunting the Red Partridge)[1]

The text is not extensive, having served in original editions to explain and complement a series of photographs. In the *Complete Works,* without illustrations, *Hunting the Red Partridge* occupies only some twenty pages. It is not so much a treatise on the technicalities of hunting this wily, native Castilian game bird as a semilyric exposé of the reasons for hunting it, an explanation of why it is the most satisfactory prey from Delibes' point of view. Like the long essay of Ortega prefacing a book on hunting by the Count of Yepes, this is primarily an exploration of motivations.

Aside from what it offers in the way of intimate insights into Delibes' feelings for his avocation, the brief text is notable for the character of Juan Gualberto, "el Barbas," a seventy-year-old Castilian of peasant stock, a brusque and hardy supposed hunting acquaintance and interlocutor of the narrator or central consciousness (identical with Delibes). *Hunting the Red Partridge* anticipates in a number of ways the next, longer work on hunting, *El libro de la caza menor,* with its shared references to Ortega, the common concern for the preservation and conservation of habitats and species, and preference for the so-called red partridge. Considerable repetition of themes, and at times of whole passages, is found in the longer work.

II El libro de la caza menor (Small Game Hunting)[2]

Considering the nature of this book, Delibes has been pleasantly surprised at its popularity, for he wrote it with no thought of profit, but simply to denounce certain menaces: the progressive disappearance of certain species, practices such as organized poaching, egg stealing, the destruction of breeding areas, and large-scale game law violations, which threaten the annihilation of the game and hence of the sport. Delibes presents a plea for more energetic measures to preserve flora and fauna from extermination, and for a sane exercise of self-control. The specific impetus behind *Small Game Hunting* was his realization, during the 1963-64 season, that available game had decreased to approximately half the level of the previous season, due in large measure to illegal shooting, increased tourism, and the killing of game for commerce. Delibes argues that the existing means of preventing marauding belong to the time of oxcarts and are totally inadequate today, and issues an appeal to all lovers of the hunt to unite in seeking better protective legislation.

Insofar as the technicalities are concerned, Delibes makes no attempt to attract the aristocrat with instructions for organizing a hunting trip or fox hunt, but simply discusses one humble, primitive, and modest form of the sport, small game hunting on foot. He has illustrous antecedents, some of which he cites, ranging from Alfonso X of Castile and Don Juan Manuel in the late Middle Ages, and continuing down to the twentieth-century philosopher, José Ortega y Gasset. Delibes, thoroughly familiar with the latter's writings on hunting, agrees in essence with his conclusion that a prime motivation for the hunter is the escape from cares of the present through becoming temporarily "paleolithic."

Delibes points out that hunting is a dynamic diversion, especially in contrast to the major alternatives for weekend amusement in Spain, spectator sports, soccer, and the bullfights (a theme also treated in *Hunting the Red Partridge*). While he gives due attention to its inconveniences—predawn rising in inclement weather; long, hard walks; cold meals in wintry fields; rain; the sudden storm and heat of late summer—the author asserts that for the true hunter, each obstacle is transformed into a new attraction. Hunting is portrayed by Delibes as an all-absorbing passion. While *Small Game Hunting* is technically in the third person, its sense is often first person. Wherever Delibes has written "The Hunter," the reader may substitute the name of the novelist. There are sections devoted to other species of small game—the quail, rabbit, hare, doves, ducks, fox, eagle, and lesser birds—but it is obvious from the proportional space allotted that "The Hunter's" great favorite is the partridge, just as in the earlier work devoted exclusively to this astute feathered prey. While the longer work is less clearly structured than *Hunting the Red Partridge* (which is in the form of conversations during a hunting trip), there is a loose ordering of topics according to the hunting seasons, beginning with the first day's excitement, the opening of the quail season in late summer, the later periods for partridge, hare, and others, following through until the close of all hunting activity. For each species, there are sections on its defensive strategy, evincing Delibes' close observation of flora and fauna. In addition to a number of autobiographical incidents in the sections recounting the first and last days of the season, this book provides further insight into the composition of *Diary of a Hunter*. It is strongly suggested that Antonio Merino, a hunting companion of Delibes who figures prominently in *Small Game Hunting*, is the prototype for Lorenzo's friend Melecio. Stylistically, too, this work often recalls the *Diary of a Hunter*, although it does not contain the whole colorful lexicon of Lorenzo.

Con la escopeta al hombro (Shouldering the Gun), yet another volume of collected essays combining observations on the hunt, on various prey and their habits with personal musings and reminiscences, was published by Destino (Barcelona: 1970) when the present book was already in press. Its overall nature is sufficiently similar to that of *Small Game Hunting* to allow omission of any detailed treatment here.

III   Vivir al día (Living from Day to Day)[3]

This volume contains some sixty miscellaneous articles written by Delibes for newspaper publication over the period from 1953 to 1967, and discusses a broad range of interests and preoccupations. The author's Prologue indicates that these are not all his newspaper articles for those fifteen years, but perhaps one-third of them, ordered chronologically. Each is followed by the date or the year of appearance, and while they do not constitute a complete intellectual diary, the collection may throw occasional light on Delibes' state of mind during the gestation of his other works. Certain articles, for instance, are particularly relevant to the genesis of *The Rats*.

There is some small autobiographical content in a few of the articles, for example, "Don Alvaro o la fuerza de la maldicencia" ("Don Alvaro or the Power of Slander"), written on the five hundredth anniversary of the execution of Don Alvaro de Luna. Delibes recalls how, as a child learning by rote the history of Valladolid, he was haunted by the gruesome drawings of the death of the one-time favorite of Juan II. This is identified as Delibes' first contact with death. The balance of the essay recreates the itinerary of Don Alvaro (somewhat in the fashion of Azorín) during the journey to Valladolid for execution. Other articles include critiques of the cinema and theater, a description of the Manchegan landscape, and reflections on the situation of the professional writer in Spain. The latter bears upon the title, which alludes to the hand-to-mouth existence of those who attempt to live by the pen, "living from day to day." Delibes' temporizing tolerance comes to the fore in "El ingenio y el ingeniero" ("Ingenuity and Engineers"), which deals with the problems created by argumentation and polemics, and "Un viajero de tercera" ("A Third-Class Traveler") expressing his sincere admiration for Albert Schweitzer. "La crisis de la didáctica" ("The Crisis of Didacticism") expounds Delibes' thoughts on pedagogy, against pedantry and rote learning. He recalls the confusion created in his youthful mind upon having to memorize interminable lists of historical figures (such as the Gothic kings) with no indication of relative importance. A related essay criticizes the forced election Spanish students must make in the college preparatory stage between sciences and the humanities, resulting in a subsequent total divorce between the man of numbers and the man of letters.

If one considers numerical weight, one of the most important categories consists of articles bearing upon the national sport of soccer; these are usually not chronicles of specific contests, but sociological considerations. Delibes' personal interests are reflected by the articles on fishing and hunting, literature and literary prizes. One especially lengthy essay describes the awarding of the 1957 Nadal Prize to another resident of Valladolid, and a friend of Delibes, Father José Luis Martín Descalzo. Several articles commemorating the deaths of fellow writers strike a midpoint between literary commentary and necrology. "Aviso a los padres de familia numerosa" ("Warning to Fathers of Large Families") satirizes Spanish red tape, while "El hombre que llovía demasiado" ("The Man Who Rained Too Much") is a humorous fantasy on the possible consequences of weather control. Delibes also touches upon religious subjects, including Holy Week processions, falsely spectacular charity, and pays tribute to the author of a weekly religious column. Such typically Spanish subjects as the custom of the siesta, the national fiesta (bullfights), and recommendations or "influence" are scrutinized, while the author's interest in death and the handling thereof results in a discussion of the desirability of simplifying the mourning and burial formalities.

Delibes usually avoids literary theorizing, but in "La novela abstracta" ("The Abstract Novel"), written apropos of *Mobile* by the French novelist, Michel Butor, he inserts certain of his own ideas on the "antinovel" and the Objectivist movement, which implicitly throw light on why he has maintained his distance from these currents. For Delibes, the so-called abstract novel is a work "without man and without sentiment, the novel of objects, but without an objective."[4] He is stupefied and dismayed to find intelligent people whom he knows and respects cultivating a literary form which to him is senseless, pretending to offer the pleasures of abstract or nonrepresentational art, but without color, through typography. Delibes observes that mental uniformity has reached such a point that there are scarcely men, only herds, and that the cultivators of the antinovel are faithful to the society in which they live insofar as they reflect its amorphous, headless nature. Nevertheless, despite these initial negative reactions, parts of his essay seem to anticipate and describe in advance aspects (although probably ironic) of his most recent work, *Parábola del Náufrago (Parable of the Drowning Man)*. "Words, with all their defects, with all the possibilities of misunderstanding which their interpretation involves, have been heretofore the most exact means of communication between men. Is it justifiable, because men do not understand each other, to desert words, decompose them, void them of all sense and propose for the reader a mental exercise in mere typographical variety of symbols?"[5] This is one thing done by the protagonist of Delibes' latest novel, albeit as a symptom of personality disintegration, and perhaps a satire or parody of the "new novel" techniques.

Among the volume's most significant articles are those bearing on the plight of Castilian villages, the misery of the countryside, and the need for agricultural reforms. As these relate directly to the pre-occupations which produced *The Rats,* and were written at roughly the same time, they will be discussed together with that novel. Included are

"La cara lavada" ("A Face Washing"), "Los pueblos moribundos" ("Moribund Villages"), "La ruina de Castilla" ("The Ruination of Castile"), and "Castilla negra y Castilla blanca" ("Black and White Castile").

IV Viejas historias de Castilla la Vieja (Old Tales of Old Castile)[6]

A few years ago the Spanish government's Ministry of Tourism promoted the publication of travel guides covering each of the country's fifty provinces. These were to be profusely illustrated and provided with texts by leading writers, who would discuss the history, peculiarities and picturesqueness of their native regions. Delibes was commissioned to do the text for the tourist guide on Castile. Instead of devoting himself to a survey of romantically ruined castles, he concentrated on the ruined lands, the poverty-stricken villages, and their miserable inhabitants. The photographer, taken by Delibes to areas the average tourist never sees, obtained magnificently eloquent photographs. Too eloquent, for the Ministery of Tourism had done its best to conceal these sores, and Delibes' "tourist guide" was rejected. With certain modifications, it was published elsewhere, first in a limited, deluxe edition (always treated more gently by the censors, since this type of edition does not reach the general public), under the title *Castilla*,[7] and subsequently reissued in a more moderately priced format with the title *Viejas historias de Castilla la Vieja*. For the person with time to read only one work of Delibes, the one which would unquestionably give the most typical and authentic picture of the novelist and his preoccupations is this brief portrait of backgrounds and surroundings without which no work of Delibes can be fully understood.

The first-person narrative is told from the perspective of a former inhabitant of a village, perhaps the same as that in *The Rats*, but in any case, definitely in the same area, for it has many of the same geographical features: "Cerro Fortuna" ("Fortune Hill"), "El soto de los Encapuchados" ("Capuchin Grove"), "Las Piedras Negras" ("The Black Rocks"), and others. The old man has returned after forty-eight years to find everything exactly as he left it, with the dust from the last threshing still on the adobe walls. While the prose expressing his recognition is lyric, this is a statement of the fact that time, in the meaningful sense, does not pass in Castile's forgotten villages; they have somehow been left at the margin of history, and to enter them is to step from the twentieth century into the Middle Ages. And this may be picturesque for the person who does not have to live there, who is unaware of what it means in terms of suffering and the loss of human potential, but Delibes is aware—perhaps more so than the villagers themselves, brutalized by conditions and ignorant that anything better exists. At the same time, he is able to perceive the peace offered by this type of life, in contrast to the hustle and bustle of modern, mechanized civilizations, and to appreciate the stolid virtues of the villagers. He understands the enormous attraction of the soil, the locale of their ancestors, which the spot of origin exercises for those born in the villages, and this imparts an occasional lyricism to descriptions of the poverty and decay.

Under the guise of the memoirs or recollections of the narrator-central consciousness, Delibes presents many typical characteristics of the villages. While it is no longer so easy as it once was in the United States to distinguish the farm or village dweller from those of urban areas, in Spain the physical appearances still suffice. Apparently the difference was more marked a generation or two ago. Isidro, narrator of *Old Tales . . . ,* was "ashamed of being from a village, and that the teachers should ask me (without questioning first whether I was from village or city), 'Isidro, from which village are you?' And it also mortified me that the other students elbowed each other and whispered, 'Have you noticed what a bumpkin's face Isidro has?' and I was careful to avoid saying 'Back in my village . . .'"

Encountering many prejudices, Isidro began to think that being a villager was something of a disgrace, and his one ambition was to lose the mark of the village which had branded him for life. However, after having gone to Bilbao (typifying the forced emigration), he worked in various jobs and eventually began to lose his shame and even to talk of the customs of his village. "And I began to realize that being from a village was a gift of God, and being from the city a bit like being a prisoner, and that the hilltops and the stork's nest and the poplars and the river were always the same, while the piles of brick and blocks of cement and mountains of stone of the city changed each day, and with the years, not one witness remained of one's birth, for while the village remained the same, the city disintegrated because of 'progress' and planning for the future." Delibes' intuition of the power the village exercises over its long-absent sons is not devoid of sympathy.

The villagers are laconic: " . . . in my village, things are not given too much importance, and if someone leaves, he will be back; and if someone gets sick, he will get well; and if he doesn't, then let him die and be buried. After all, the village goes on, and something of one remains, adhering to the hillocks, the poplars and the stubble. In the cities, one dies completely; in the villages, no . . ." Looking back upon his childhood, and alternating with memories of the disputes between his parents over his father's drinking, he remembers the arrival of electricity, and the reaction in the village: hysteria in some, resentment in others, and insistence that it had ruined the crop of certain trees, even though this was almost inevitably spoiled by late freezes. "In my village, the seasons don't take things seriously, and summer and spring and autumn and winter cross and recross without the slightest regard. There is just as likely to be a heat wave in February as snow in May. And if it freezes after St. Ciriaco, when the trees have budded, they are sort of burned, and there is nothing to do but wait until next year."

Via this matter-of-fact and understated acceptance of the harsh Castilian climate which is the true protagonist of *The Rats,* the reader comes to intuit that here, starvation is a way of life. "The high plain is an immense, desolate expanse, and on cloudy days, the land looks like the sky and the sky like the land, both equally unfurnished and uninviting. When I was born, the high plain had neither beginning nor end, no interruptions or points of reference. It was so harshly open and arduous that just looking at it tired the eyes. Then they brought the light from Navalejos, and the high-tension poles sprang up in it like squalid giants." Delibes' description of the steppe-like panorama of the Tierra de Campos at times nears the epic, mythic tone of Antonio Machado's *La tierra de Alvargonzález,* reduced to colloquial language.

The pull of the land and tradition are strong for the peasant mentality, and despite frequently miserable conditions, there is fierce individual resistance to emigration or other changes in the ancestral patterns. Isidro did not want to work in the fields, so his father gave him a beating and tied him to a bed post without food or water for forty-eight hours. The mature Isidro looks back without resentment, almost with amusement, which reflects the still-extant patriarchal system, and the feeling that the lands somehow justify the harshest measures. Thus, the Hernando brothers, who had found the secret of better wheat crops, guarded the knowledge so jealously that the youngest Hernando would shoot at those who attempted to spy upon them at work in their fields. Local superstitions and folklore also find their way into the pages of *Old Tales.* The strongly-rooted idea that certain waters of the area have healthful properties, serving to cure eczema, boils, psoriasis, and various other skin infections, is a belief not shaken by failures in specific cases.

The admixture of superstition and religion in rural Castile produces a veritable plethora of home-grown "saints," so that rare is the village without one of its own. Monotony, a day-to-day existence with hardly a change in generations, seems to provoke as a reaction the tendency to see the miraculous in what is even slightly out of the ordinary. This Delibes subtly satirizes in the amusing, archetypical account of the "martyr," Sisinia, who dies defending her virtue and immediately became something of a local legend. The cause for her sainthood was espoused by the priest, who should have known better if the villagers did not, but insisted on seeing miracles where there was nothing even faintly extraordinary.

The "miracles" or favors of Sisinia to her followers are a comic litany of rural credulity. One day Zenona, lacking money to reroof the dovecote, appealed to Sisinia, and the following day collected three years' back rent on a piece of land (one cheese and six measures of wheat), which sufficed to acquire the dozen necessary tiles. Ponciano, who needed a screw for his plow, found one in the haycart. Although rusty and twisted, it could be straightened and used. This grace was also obtained after allegedly commending the matter to Sisinia. A hunter claimed he was favored with her intercession in finding a partridge despite his dog's being sick with distemper. The foregoing persons and others equally blessed contributed to a fund for the beatification of Sisinia, started by the priest, whose most lucrative contribution came because the gift of speech was restored to a parrot, previously mute for three months, as a result of the intercession of the "martyr." While these figure among the most amusing pages of Delibes, they reflect a thoroughly medieval outlook, tragic in the present day, particularly when transplanted beyond the villages. And existence is pitiably close to the limits of survival when one rusty screw can be a cause for prayer and rejoicing.

Isidro's description of the courting customs in his village is also amusing. The "Lovers' Trees" were traditionally reserved for declarations, so a young man with marriage on his mind had only to sit under these trees with the object of his affections for her to answer yes or no. The custom allegedly arose because of the extreme timidity of the villagers, although Isidro remarks that despite the timidity in proposals, several children were conceived under the "Lovers' Trees." He himself never married, because during strolls in the years before leaving the village, he always found the space occupied and so never proposed to the girl chosen by his aunt. He thus felt no compunction or responsibility upon leaving the village.

The lands belonging to the village, viewed from "Fortune Hill," appear like a sea, an unbroken expanse, grey in winter, green in spring, yellow in summer, and ochre in autumn, but always a sea, stretching away to the horizon without a ripple. The area's harsh climate produced wheat stalks so strong and sharp that children were allegedly forbidden to walk among them, as some had lost eyes. Many descriptions of the climate have an epic ring, and there is a stark lyricism in the changing flocks of birds that follow the round of seasons. Delibes' observations of the habits of birds produce an interesting account of how crows "hold court," judging and immediately executing the accused, who does not resist. The "Black Rocks" are a geological curiosity in the area, dating from the last Ice Age, and the "Mesa of the Dead" is associated with the superstition that whoever plows its top would die as soon as the crop began to ripen. However, the man who took the risk not only survived, but was able to harvest a yearly crop, while surrounding lands were so impoverished that they could only be cultivated in alternate years.

Nearing his village, the returning emigrant is beset by fears that things will have changed, and inquires of a youth if tractors have arrived. The boy replies that to buy even one, they would have to sell the entire area. Isidro perceives the familiar landmarks, all unchanged, everything with the same biblical character of half a century before. Back in the village, he finds that only the men have changed: they are the sons and grandsons of those he knew, but nothing else is altered. His house is exactly as he left it, the scene is identical, except that his "little" sisters now have white hair. The repetition of these two scenes separated by a lifetime is a powerful method of bringing home to the reader the sameness of existence in the villages, the almost total lack of progress, the nearly indescribable backwardness produced by the combination of extreme poverty and resistance to change.

While the returning native son may rejoice to find that time has left so little mark, it should not be concluded that this is Delibes' attitude. Some critics who have misunderstood this, willfully or otherwise, condemn him for being reactionary, skeptical of progress, and shocked that in some parts of the world people no longer live in caves.[8] This exaggeration is perhaps due to professional jealousy; no such sweeping generalization can be defended, although legitimate confusion may result from a certain ambivalence in Delibes himself. He does not condemn the conditions described in the villages, although not from blind optimism or because of being a pro-government propagandist as the above critic implies; rather it is because if he did condemn, that would be propaganda, simply of another shade, and Delibes is too much of an artist to confuse literature and indoctrination.

The text just discussed, as observed before, was written as a "tourist guide" and rejected because of its emphasis on the backwardness and poverty the government wished to camouflage in the interests of tourism. Counterbalancing his negative observations, Delibes recognizes the positive aspects of rural existence, the relative peace of mind, the preservation of old-time virtues, traditional values, and simple pleasures. Nevertheless, he does not feel that these should be purchased at the price of an empty stomach, privation, and suffering, conditions which only progress can eradicate. Castile's plight is longstanding, a problem of generations or centuries, but it has been aggravated in recent times by catastrophic weather. Six or seven consecutive years of agricultural disasters, beginning in 1959, so accelerated the rate of emigration that Delibes expressed the fear that Castile would become a wasteland, uncultivated and uninhabited, strewn with the ruins of abandoned villages and deserted fields. This danger, together with humanitarian considerations, inspired his energetic campaign for reform. There is no doubt as to his having chosen "progress," whatever its negative consequences.

CHAPTER 10

The Plight of Castile

T HE "discovery" of Castile as a literary theme is usually considered the achievement of the Generation of '98, with perhaps the most significant discoverers being Azorín, Unamuno, and Antonio Machado—none of them Castilians. Later, Ortega attempted an interpretation of Castile, and thereafter the theme went into literary eclipse until the postwar era, when it again acquires the dimensions of an obsession for two outstanding contemporary novelists, Delibes and Ana María Matute.

There are numerous differences in Delibes' vision of Castile and that of his predecessors, an obvious but important one being the nature and depth of individual acquaintance with the subject. None of the previous writers most eloquent in descriptions and interpretations of Castile was born there, and they saw Spain's heartland with eyes quite different from the native son's. They were, in fact, most often writing of both times and landscapes to which they did not belong. Many pages have been devoted to investigating Azorín's treatment of Castile, and while his work is beautiful, he did see the area with the eyes of an aesthete. Antonio Vilanova, in an article apropos of *The Rats,* makes passing mention of Delibes' deep love for the customs and the people of Castile, "which prevents his adopting the more or less indifferent and superior attitude of the men of 1898, for whom, as Laín Entralgo said, the inhabitant of the Iberian countryside is a blot on the landscape." [1]

For Azorín the crumbling villages and arid lands were not a critical human dilemma, an almost insoluble ecological problem, but a panorama softened and beautified by the patina of history, still alive just beneath the surface and awaiting evocation. Unamuno's writings on Castile contain love and identification with the region, but it is frequently contrasted with his native Bilbao, greener and less austere. And Unamuno was interested primarily in what Castile symbolized of the national spirit, the Spanish "essence," and as such, a possible key to the peninsular character and destiny. These writers in general conceived the area as a symbolic concentration of what was most Spanish, as an historical entity inseparably associated with the moments of greatest glory. Thus, it became a sort of mystical access to the past on the one hand, and to the future on the other. Castile was not viewed in terms of the here and now, realistically, but somewhat platonically, as an abstract, spiritual concept, intuited more than observed.

Delibes, despite occasional idealization of aspects of the simple country life, sees Castile with the utmost realism, neither as the link with a once-glorious past, nor as distilled essence of Spain. His Castile is a concrete, geographic, socio-economic complex, problematic in many ways, very much within the here and now. The Castilian landscape is not a literary motif for him, nor an aesthetic perspective, but a lived reality, inseparable from the men who inhabit it, and whose destinies it controls.

Delibes is by no means unaware of Castilian history, which is one of his areas of specialization, but he does not delve into bygone eras in his writing. And while fully aware of the implications of Castile's geography, its specific determinism, he does not attempt to derive from the geographical austerity corresponding traits in the national character, as had Unamuno. Delibes does relate the climatic harshness and unpredictability to disastrous agricultural and economic conditions, portraying the stoicism, tenacity, and occasional primitivism of peasants still bound to the soil, but does not generalize the effects of geography and climate on the national character. Nor does he even attempt to postulate an abstract national or regional personality, but limits his focus to individual cases, albeit at time archetypical.

Of all the writers of the Generation of '98, Delibes is closest to Antonio Machado, the Machado of *Campos de Castilla* and the *Tierra de Alvargonzález,* and both were acutely aware of the harshness and brutalizing misery of the land even while deeply moved by its stark beauty. It may be significant that the area near Soria, described by Machado, is not far from the section portrayed by Delibes, with many similar climatic and geographic characteristics, though Soria is more mountainous. The figure of the silent, poverty-ridden peasant, a gigantic, black silhouette which haunts Machado's verses, is a direct link to Delibes, and both are notably sensitive to the subtle, muted colorings and the occasional isolated, stark vertical forms of trees or steeples thrusting upward in the horizonal emptiness. Machado, too, was most aware of the humble flora and fauna of the region, and both writers find beauty in the lowly plants and birds overlooked in more "artistic" treatments. Delibes' critics have mentioned the tenderness and lyricism softening his harsh vision, a poetic quality which also links him to Machado, and the prose of Azorín, with whom he has been compared in conciseness and precision. But Delibes could never limit himself to paintings of the landscape, or *costumbrista* description of rural life, more than picturesque scenes for him, a dramatic misery which cannot be portrayed with aesthetic indifference or simple pity.

The earlier approach to Castile was more theoretical, general, and abstract, dissociated from concrete problems and inequities, and any solutions derived tended to be vague and not easily reduced to practice: reviving the spiritual vigor of the country, becoming new Don Quijotes, and the like. Postwar writers usually lack the philosophical, generalized dimension, and are inspired by the zeal of the social reformer rather than the sensibility of the artist. While the Generation of '98 was led by concern for Spain's problems beyond normal bounds of creative literature into philosophy, the present generation exceeds those limits in the directions of journalism and sociology. Delibes in this is entirely typical of the spirit of his times.

In thoroughgoing acquaintance with the landscape acquired during a lifetime as an avid sportsman, Delibes exceeds the familiarity acquired in walking jaunts by Unamuno and Machado, or the travels of Azorín. As a lifelong resident, he is aware of the area's peculiarities, without finding in them the exoticism that attracted some of the Generation of '98. The sad, dusty, forgotten villages represent something more immediate than the static survival of a decrepit, ruined past. His vision is thus less "literary" and more concretely localized, with greater concern for the problematic present and future than with the past, or the "soul." Castile is ever-present in his writing, except for the travel books, and even in these (as in *The Diary of an Emigrant,* his one novel set largely outside the region), its memory hovers obsessively in the background.

Delibes' works on Castile can be divided into two groups, the rural and urban, with the former being more eloquent, original, and memorable, perhaps more typical of his individual style and preoccupations. Except for *The Cypress,* set in Avila, the urban novels deal with Valladolid, underscoring the stagnant, unimaginative nature of the economy, the poverty and misery of many as contrasted with the comfort of a few. Even with today's postwar industrialization, Valladolid has a shockingly large number of beggars who have not been eradicated by government campaigns against mendicants. Poverty, want, misery, and almost subhuman conditions of existence are repeatedly portrayed by Delibes in both rural and urban settings, the results of a combination of poor natural resources and centuries of exploitation and neglect by the central government. The protagonists of three of the Valladolid novels live close to the starvation level: the specter of hunger, want, and insecurity haunts *Still It Is Day* and *The Red Leaf,* while Lorenzo in *The Diary of a Hunter* is definitely lower class and forced to seek extra part-time employment. The only exception to a seemingly general trend among Delibes' protagonists is the wealthy merchant, Cecilio Rubes of *My Adored Son Sisí.* In *Five Hours with Mario,* which presumably takes place also in Valladolid, there are few exterior details, but the economic preoccupations of Mario's widow do not leave her mind even while she keeps vigil beside his body. *Parable of the Drowning Man* has an urban setting, but some characteristics suggest Madrid. Again, physical detail is minimal; elements of fantasy or hallucination supplant the portrayal of identifiable geography.

It is not so much in Delibes' treatment of the city, however, as of smaller villages and the countryside that it is possible to recognize a new and individual voice speaking of Castile. Examples are found in the collection of short novels, *Siestas with the Southern Breeze,* in parts of The *Diary of a Hunter* and *The Red Leaf,* in the hunting and miscellaneous works, and especially in *Old Tales of Old Castile,* and the much-honored novel, *The Rats.* For Delibes, the essence of Castile is concentrated in a vast semidesert beginning some fifteen miles north of Valladolid, the "Tierra de Campos," described in an unpublished lecture: "... this is the living image of arid Castile, of Castile spectacular precisely for its lack of decoration, its total absence of the spectacular. Desolation: that is the drama, and consequently the fascinating spectacle. The nudity, the barrenness, the rocky hills, the sterile washes, the half-dozen poplars following the trickle of an arroyo, the bare rises punctuated by a few rickety almonds, the sinister holm oak crowning the ashy butte ... this is the Tierra de Campos, and therefore, Castile."

The novelist emphasizes the importance of the heavens, not simply part of the landscape where sky meets earth at the horizon, but an ever-present factor in the economy, source of drought or flood, welcome rain or unseasonable heat and cold, determiner of feast or famine. He stresses the proverbially negative climate, Castile's capricious atmospheric phenomena reflected in numerous folk sayings. Popular refrains related to the *santoral* (Saints' calendar), which in rural areas replaces dates, reflect similar preoccupations, and Delibes makes frequent use of this as well. These folkloric elements attest his familiarity with the rural lexicon, an acquaintance much greater than that of his literary predecessors, and his mature works constitute veritable treasure-houses of rural dialect, expressions, and lore.

Castile is seen as essentially bypassed by civilization, funereally static: "Nothing fundamental has changed in desolate Castile in the past century,"[2] yet despite backwardness and poverty, Delibes sees also "a pool of peace in the whirlpool of mechanization." It is perhaps the last refuge of self-sufficiency or rugged individualism. But these positive notes contrast with many negative ones: primitive forms of life survive, and in mid-twentieth century the methods of cultivation are thousands of years old, the result of poverty, the abrupt land, and suspicious rural traditionalism. Such primitive conditions favor the incidence of primitive mentalities, and Delibes' gallery of characters includes some of the most elemental personalities in all of Spanish literature, barely human or subhuman examples of isolation, deprivation, and mental retardation, such as tío Ratero in *The Rats* and the younger Nilo in "The Walnut Trees." The villages, in harmony with the countryside, are bereft of health and sanitary facilities, often reached only on foot, without paved streets, electricity, or communications, their houses of adobe or mud—existence has hardly changed since the construction of the ruined castles dotting the landscape. The land goes seasonally from mud to dust, and recently the population has declined as the younger generation flees the miserable, malodorous, constricted environment. But little else has changed. While comprehending the need for emigration, Delibes laments the desolation left behind, the idle lands and deserted villages with sometimes only those too old to leave awaiting death in the silent doorways: "Cortiguera is a village near Burgos in the process of disappearance. Among its abandoned stone houses, many with coats of arms, live two old couples and two ancient widows. It is a dying village, agonizing. Its tortuous streets, invaded by weeds and nettles, without a dog's bark or a child's laugh to break the silence, enclose a pathetic gravity, the lugubrious air of a cemetery . . ."[3] Delibes also fears for the emigrants, feeling that the villager, morally, materially, and mentally primitive, is unprepared to face twentieth-century life, even in the diluted form found in Spain. Nevertheless, he sympathizes with the reasons of the young for not wishing to continue in the villages: "Cortiguera is a village without a road, without a railway, without telephones or cultural centers, sports, or even dancing, and of course without television, and youth today is justifiably not interested in anonymous sacrifices, useless heroism, and unrequited effort." The few old people remaining have often nearly forgotten how to relate to other human beings.

I   Las ratas (The Rats)[4]

The village of *The Rats* has not been quite so depleted by emigration as some others portrayed by Delibes, but the conditions are present: poverty, the absence of modern conveniences, a bare survival level of existence, exhausted lands, and cruel climate. A number of abandoned houses attest the exodus that has already begun. The rats of the title are a staple in the diet of the cave dwellers and some villagers, a detail which among some of Delibes' readers aroused protests and accusations of exaggeration or excessive bitterness. Delibes replied that "anyone who knows even superficially the life of small Castilian villages can testify that I have not been guilty of the slightest exaggeration."[5] In an interview with Jesús Mora, he states that tío Ratero had a real-life prototype, a man living in a village of Cuéllar (not far north of Valladolid) who hunts rats, eating and selling them to survive.[6]

In the *Complete Works, The Rats* is included in Volume Three. Delibes notes in his Prologue that a principal concern is solitude; the solitude of the child protagonist, el Nini; his father, tío Ratero; and the neighboring villagers, without exceptions. Their solitude is of a different quality, however, than that of characters in the other novels in this volume, *Still It Is Day* and *The Red Leaf,* lonely in the midst of the city. The villagers' solitude is not due simply to lack of human warmth and affection as in the other two works; it is also a physical solitude, in a hostile environment, and a symbolic solitude, signifying the neglect of the central government and the forgetfulness of society around them. It is not merely a mental attitude; it is also an objective fact.

Like Delibes' more recent novels, *The Rats* is loosely structured, essentially a novel without a plot, composed of a series of anecdotes held together by the personality of el Nini, who also serves as central consciousness in parts of the narrative, constituting one of Delibes' more extensive utilizations of the technique of the point of view. While there is humor, satire, and caricature, the central situation and events are anything but funny, tragic in their insolubility. One specific inspiration for the novel was a government campaign in 1960 to clean and whitewash the villages, at least those on the major highways, so they would not shock and disgust the tourists. It apparently was also attempted to end cave dwelling so tourists would not subsequently tell that Spaniards still lived in caves. The village of *The Rats* is located on the provincial highway, and the novel ostensibly revolves around the mayor's attempt to dislodge tío Ratero from his cave, although an equally important conflict is man's struggle with nature. In an article written apropos of the cleanup campaign, some two years before publication of *The Rats,* Delibes expressed criticism that rather than any desire for hygiene, the real motive was that the extremes of misery would not be revealed, suggesting that "before painting the exterior of these villages, it would be better to study their interior and try to discover the cause of such shameful scars . . . perhaps studying the administration and the socio-economic factors and modifying these, we could better improve their appearance . . ."[7]

The text of *The Rats* is preceded by a sketch of the area, showing the village, road, river, fields, and the location of the caves in the surrounding hills. One critic compared this to a similar technique of Faulkner. The landscape is so poor and barren that each feature has a name, every hill and dovecote is as familiar as the human faces of the community. The hamlet and its inhabitants figure prominently, but the novel's protagonists live in a hillside cave, with the boy coming down to the village frequently to do odd jobs. El Nini is a strange child of perhaps eleven, who despite the most sordid environment and strongly negative heredity, has a superior, almost clairvoyant intelligence. The parallel between this boy and the child Jesus is repeatedly suggested: by a biblical citation prefacing the novel, and by scenes wherein el Nini amazes his elders with his wisdom, as well as explicit comparisons made by villagers with Jesus in the temple. It was not Delibes' intention, of course, to write a religious satire; rather, this device underlines the human worth and dignity of all men, regardless of their circumstances, and the importance of saving the children, who represent the future. In the interview previously cited, Delibes stated that el Nini "symbolizes purity and generosity, qualities becoming all too rare in our time . . . (He represents) the man who gives of himself," and as such was intended to have a universal validity. In another interview in 1965, Delibes defined a religious man as "one who gives of himself without reserve to his fellowman, without any hope of compensation."[8] Such is more often than not the case of el Nini, who has been considered "one of the greatest creations of Delibes. His mentality and reactions are

perfectly adapted to the world in which he lives."[9] The same observer
calls attention to the boy's "almost sensual intimacy with Nature."

The cave inhabited by el Nini and his father, tío Ratero, is
apparently bare of furnishings except a heap of straw, where the two
sleep with the dog, Fa. Tío Ratero lives by hunting rats, which he sells
to the tavernkeeper, Malvino, at two pesetas apiece, and occasionally to
the shepherd, Rabino. His meals, prepared in the tavern, consist of two
rats fried and sprinkled with vinegar, wine, and bread. The remaining
rats are presumably consumed by other patrons of Malvino; most meats
in protein-poor Spain are beyond the reach of the lower class. El Nini
also earns minimal amounts of money by helping with a variety of
tasks: slaughtering, constructing scarecrows, pruning vines, and
preparing hotbeds. His most important function, however, is as weather
prophet and minor seer, advising the villagers when to sow and reap,
when to butcher and to perform all activities depending on favorable
weather. His predictions are received as gospel, and although the boy
has no formal education, his wisdom in practical matters is proverbial.
Living in close and constant contact with nature during all seasons, he
knows the habits of animals and birds, and how to read the signs of
change. While Doña Resu, the "Eleventh Commandment," attributes
his knowledge to the devil, Delibes states that it is due entirely to his
powers of observation. It is also derived from his association with old
Rufo, the "Centenarian," from whom he has learned proverbs, tales,
and recent history. His grandfathers imparted practical knowledge of
flora and fauna and various tasks. He knows little, however, of things
not related to nature, and when asked about the rich man's ailing
tractor, replied, "I don't know; that's invented."

The family tree of el Nini is something of a mystery even to the family.
His grandmother, Iluminada, lived with two brothers, Román and
Abundio, all in the same cave. It is not known which of them fathered
the mentally retarded tío Ratero and his sister (or half-sister) Marcela,
the mother of el Nini, confined to an insane asylum some four years
earlier. The grandmother and one grandfather have died, and the other
disappeared, abandoning their cave. Gypsies who lived in a third cave
accepted a low-rent house in the village, but even the approximately
two dollars a month involved is a fortune in the eyes of tío Ratero,
who insists "the cave is mine," and resists all efforts of the authorities
to evacuate the province's last cave. The conflict of the individual
versus society, suggested in several of Delibes' works, receives a
strength of presentation exceeded only in *Parable of the Drowning*

Man. Intervention by the state is seen as a necessary evil in *The Rats,* given the subhuman conditions, but nevertheless an evil, taking its toll of those who, like tío Ratero, are unprepared to exist in the "modern" world. The gap between life in the caves and in the village parallels an even greater gulf between rural areas and the cities, making of emigration a human drama and not merely an economic problem.

Almost every villager has a nickname, variously serving to characterize, describe, or ridicule, in a fashion typifying small-town cruelty. Monosyllabic names or simplified forms (Fa, el Nini) indicate the elementary nature of mentalities. Other nicknames are generic, based upon the social function: the manager, the mayor, the rich man, the poacher, and tío Ratero, whose real name is unknown—he is known exclusively as the rat hunter. The tag line technique begun in *The Path* is employed extensively in *The Rats.* Repetition is frequent, both of phrases and incidents, serving to intensify the character presentation and underscore the dramatic starkness. Tío Ratero is allegedly incapable of pronouncing more than four words at a time, and these of extreme simplicity. The only concept well developed in his mind is that of private property; his conversation consists largely of affirmations that "The cave is mine," "The rats are mine," and "Nini is mine." The symbolic implications of this character are subtly emphasized by Delibes' use of light and shadow. Tío Ratero is almost always glimpsed in the darkness of the cave, or seen against the light, silhouetted as a dark shadow. This gives the descriptions the quality of an etching, with the same rigorous austerity of composition, lucidity, and economy of line. Most figures are characterized by their manias, limitations, and picturesque quirks, sometimes amusing, sometimes pathetic.

Tío Ratero's main preoccupation is another rat hunter from the neighboring village of Torrecillórigo; he believes that the other is hunting in "his" territory and killing "his" rats. This obsession is fomented by Malvino, who frequently mentions having seen this youth, Luis, although no one else sees him in the area. Tío Ratero develops an intense hate, unleashed at the end of the novel, during a bad season, when he finds Luis in "his" territory, talking with el Nini. He kills the other hunter after a bloody, hand-to-hand battle, using as the fatal weapon the iron hook employed for extracting rats from their burrows. This crime unexpectedly ends the other struggle over occupancy of the cave, for with his father in jail, the boy must be placed in an orphanage or raised by some villager, and will receive the schooling which tío Ratero had refused. While the ending can thus be seen to suggest some hope for a better future for the boy, he himself is far from happy in the moment he contemplates the corpse of his father's victim and informs him that now they must leave the cave. "They (society) won't understand," murmurs the child. Other incidents reflect the primitive, elementary violence of life in this area, such as the murder of the so-called "Rabino viejo," the one man who subscribed to Darwin's theories, by a self-appointed "religious" committee. There are numerous other examples of intolerance, religious and secular, punctuated by recollections of the assassinations, mutilations, and other atrocities of the Civil War.

As *The Rats* obtained the distinction of the Critics' Prize, signifying their judgment that it was Spain's best novel of 1962, the vast majority of secondary material available is favorable or laudatory. Francisco Umbral considers it "an important advance (in Delibes' career), and exercise in novelistic synthesis."[10] Vázquez Zamora emphasizes the beauty of the novel, despite its sordidness and misery, opining that "with all surety *(Las ratas)* will live on in Spanish literature, despite contingencies."[11] For him, the world of *The Rats* has qualities like that of Dante in its limitation of space and characters, a certain unreal time, and the atmosphere of torment. The use of the *santoral,* a calendar without dates, accentuates the feeling of timelessness, and yet does not detract from testimonial values for the here and now. Vázquez Zamora points out that there is nothing superfluous in the novel, nothing insignificant either in the narrative or in the village economy.

While a number of critics, including A. Valencia,[12] spoke of *tremendismo* in *The Rats,* the term is not really applicable. As a literary movement, *tremendismo* involves exaggeration, a negative aesthetic, distortion systematically pursued for the purpose of producing a "tremendous" reaction on the part of the reader. Some moments of violence in the novel—particularly the final scene—compare in intensity with those in classic works of *tremendismo,* such as Camilo José Cela's *La familia de Pascual Duarte,* but the prevailing atmosphere is not of violence. What is most "tremendous" in *The Rats* is what is most real and unexaggerated: the harsh struggle for life of the Castilian peasant. Living in caves and eating rats are facts, and perhaps the one exaggeration comes when Justo, the village mayor, tells the governor that "everyone in the valley" eats them, and this was not meant to be taken literally. Also, Delibes has a definite socio-political goal, while *tremendismo* had no more specific extraliterary aims than a generalized protest or cry of pain. Finally, if Delibes had kept apart from the movement in his beginnings as a writer, when it was at its height, there is little reason why he should decide to join after it had gone out of fashion.

Linguistic elements are of interest in *The Rats,* as in the *Diaries,* with much rural and agricultural terminology, regionalisms, and colloquialisms, and extensive use of the *refranero,* folk proverbs and sayings, and references to local saints. Stylistically, the economy of expression is impressive, with brief sentences, briefer dialogue, and a prose notably precise, terse, and personal. Delibes' use of a specific sublanguage, the rural dialect which he knows firsthand, enriches the story that unfolds in it. The work has a definite philological value, although the novelist is unpretentious in this regard. Critics frequently mention the sober realism and classic simplicity of *The Rats,* not only its brevity (and it might be classed as a novelette), but the limitation of characters and spatial elements. José Luis Sampedro,[13] a highly intelligent novelist and scholar, has pointed out that in Delibes' sketch preceding the text, there are exactly twenty-three "labels" designating various landscape features: hills, river, trees, caves, hillocks, meadow, fields, well, haystack, cemetery, dovecote, and highway, and that the entire novel unfolds within these limits. Time is also limited, approximately one year, beginning in late autumn and ending the following summer. For those unfamiliar with the saints whose names replace dates in the novel—and even Spanish critics complained of the unintelligibility of the saint's calendar[14] —the passage of time is perceptible only in the eternal round of seasons, in the changing colors of nature from ochre to yellow to green to gold, which contributes a sense of endless cycle and emphasizes subliminally the dependence of man upon the weather.

The Rats is more dramatic than previous works of Delibes in its brevity and intensity, and the setting, resembling a stage backdrop. It has definite elements of the "social novel," as frequently remarked by critics, and is recognized by some as one of the best of that genre.[15] Social elements are low-key but penetrating, inherent in the circumstances themselves, such as the causes underlying rat hunting. They are not manifested in stereotyped good and evil classes; Delibes does not distort one to idealize another. Nor does he offer a simple transcription of everyday conversation, like many works of this movement. He does not indulge in propaganda, nor limit himself to a grey, monotonous, impartial report, for *The Rats* has symbolic and artistic qualities usually eschewed by more radical partisans of the "social novel." Delibes stated in the previously cited interview with Jesús Mora that he did "not propose to write a *novela social,* exactly, but to expose multiple coinciding problems."

Antonio Vilanova[16] affirms that undoubtedly Delibes' most valuable contribution to the contemporary Spanish novel is having given a "new focus and a new dimension to the realistic description of life in the rural areas of Castile. His intuition of the sentiments and passions moving the soul of the farmer has nothing to do with the idyllic scenes of rural life found in the *costumbrista* novels," continues Vilanova, who proceeds to distinguish between Delibes and Pereda, with whom he was frequently compared early in his career. Delibes' love for his native province does not lead him to imitate Pereda's blindly sentimental defense of ruralism. Another interpretation of the symbolism of *The Rats* is offered by Vilanova, who sees a "symbolic incarnation of the virtues and defects of this world ... viewed from within" in el Nini and tío Ratero. For him, Nini is the "premature incarnation of the ancestral wisdom of an entire people," and tío Ratero of their hard-headed, savage stubborness, as well as a "symbol of the infrahuman condition in which rural Castilians have lived for centuries," a symbolism equally implicit in the caves still used as human dwellings, and of course, in the hunting of rats. This is a world devoid of love or tenderness, in which even sensuality seems forgotten in the daily struggle for life, a world necessarily cruel. The pathetic and grotesque drama is suddenly resolved in blood, as with savage brutality tío Ratero reacts like a wild beast. His tragedy is that of "the primitive and elementary being, pursued and surrounded by society,"[17] who responds instinctively.

Villanova calls attention to the artistic distance traveled by Delibes since *The Path,* a tenderly ironic and poetically humorous vision of a delightful mountain village, to the tragic, fatalistic, desolate, and somberly moving view of a miserable village of weeds and nettles in the desert-like wheatlands of the high plateau. In fact, the lyric tone of *The Path* has become epic in *The Rats,* the "epic of hunger" as in the picaresque novel, with which many characteristics are shared. Nature is no longer inviting, but threatening, implacable. The village of adobe is like an excrescence of the earth itself, scarcely different from the caves, with crumbling or abandoned houses, and cold winds which whip the high plains whose brown furrows stretch symmetrically to the endless horizon. This is a world governed by injustice and misery, where the majority are indifferent to the suffering of others, where resignation and fatalism have reigned since man's beginning. Unable to decide to abandon the inhospitable land of their forefathers, Castilian farmers and shepherds curse the destiny which weighs upon them. Theirs is the tragedy of a land incapable of sustaining its inhabitants.

CHAPTER 11

Cinco horas con Mario
(Five Hours with Mario)

THE first impression caused by reading *Cinco horas con Mario (Five Hours with Mario)*[1] is that of a radical change in direction, a "new" Delibes. This is due to several factors. Technically speaking, the novel is almost entirely one long interior monologue: the thoughts of Mario's widow, Carmen, during the night before burial, as she sits beside his body. The use of this technique is rare in Delibes' earlier works, and not extensive at any time. The closest antecedents occur in short stories from the year 1963, quite likely the most immediate fictional predecessors in order of composition. In "The Hawk" and "The Self-Love of Juanito Osuna," the torrential flow of words, simulating conversation and oral narrative, greatly resembles the flow of consciousness in *Five Hours with Mario*. Further similarity exists in that many of Carmen's thoughts are directed to Mario, as though she were arguing with the dead man, a silent, one-way conversation which apparently becomes audible at some point near the end, for her son enters saying that he thought he had heard her talking. The conversation in "The Self-Love . . ." presumably voiced, is likewise one-way.

Thematically, too, it might appear that Delibes has done an about-face, for while previous works seemed uniformly to uphold the institution of the family, this novel definitely implies an attack upon the sacrosanct Spanish wife and mother. The realistic, objective world, city-country, nature, popular types, and nearly all physical detail have been submerged in the subjective, replaced by the psychological exposé of Carmen from within. No previous novel by Delibes has been devoted entirely to psychological probing, and this is the first time that a female receives his primary attention. With the exception of Desi in *The Red Leaf*, the women created by Delibes have played unimportant, secondary roles, and are frequently caricatures or stereotypes.

Formal plot structure began to disappear from his works with *The Path*, but subsequent writings did follow a loose, anecdotal plan. In *Five Hours with Mario*, even anecdotes have been suppressed or so fragmented that often the reader must reconstruct them from pieces gleaned throughout the novel, putting together Carmen's disjointed thoughts and near-ravings. This is essentially a novel without action, but some sensation of movement is conveyed by the rapid time shifts in Carmen's mind from present to multiple pasts. It might be said that further movement occurs as her mind jumps from one association to another within different periods, but this "action" is essentially the same as the first, mental, emotional, and internal. Thus there is ample reason for believing that *Five Hours with Mario* represents a new artistic orientation, or at least an experiment with hitherto untried techniques.

However, Delibes has not broken completely with former patterns. *Five Hours with Mario* is not really so different from all that preceded. It is still very recognizably Delibes, with his particular vocabulary, his way of handling dialogue, his patterns of repetition, and his personal style which carry over despite altered techniques. And in a sense, the technique is simply an extension of the "point of view" used as early as *The Path*. The setting may well be Valladolid; it is a Castilian city of some size, although any clues (street, newspaper, and church names) are sufficiently vague to fit many places. The deceased shared several biographical details with Delibes: a similar age, a family of several members, a similar profession (professor and writer), social idealism; he has also an eldest son in the university, an asthenic build and temperament. This does not imply, however, that *Five Hours with Mario* is an autobiographical novel. Most importantly, the personality of Carmen is entirely different from that of Delibes' wife, and the domestic situations dominating the retrospective monologue cannot be compared. The novelist has incorporated elements from his own life, as he did in *Diary of a Hunter*, but the novel proper is fiction. Thematic links to earlier works and to the personality of Delibes appear especially in the Christian Socialist activities and economic preoccupations of Mario; these are concerns shared by the novelist.

The beginning chosen by Delibes presents certain special narrative problems. When the reader knows the end from the outset, it is sometimes difficult to achieve suspense or dramatic anticipation, and hence to maintain interest. Delibes has succeeded in this by reserving significant parts of Carmen's self-revelation, the true reason for her desire to be alone with her husband's body, until the final moment, just before dawn. Writing a novel whose presumptive protagonist is dead in the beginning is, of course, not new. Recent antecedents in Spanish include *La amortajada*[2] and *Algo pasa en la calle*.[3] The former differs in that the supposition is made that the deceased still has some faint awareness, and the narrative viewpoint is situated within the fading consciousness of the dead woman. The latter is quite similar, for the dead man, like Mario, was a liberal professor who had died suddenly in the prime of life, and in each novel the reader must reconstruct the personality of the deceased from thoughts and words of those who knew him, frequently self-serving and lacking in objectivity or beclouded by emotion. Delibes may have been unfamiliar with *La amortajada*, a Chilean novel not particularly successful in Spain, but he would likely have known *Algo pasa en la calle*, or at least its author, who won the Nadal Prize a year or two after him. While there is no question of imitation, the number of coincidences is striking. Parallels can be drawn between the personalities of the two widows, the sons, the parents-in-law, and the characters and intellectual interests of the dead men. One important difference is that Delibes concentrates on only one consciousness or perspective, one vision of Mario, while Quiroga offers five or six. Although each writer gives an extremely negative portrait of the widow, the depth and extent of Delibes' treatment are considerably greater.

There is some question as to what degree it may have been Delibes' purpose to attack the commonly-held stereotype of the idealized Spanish wife and mother. While Carmen comes off badly—she is a hypocritical social climber with a martyr complex; a frivolous, empty-headed, domineering egotist; a vain flirt possibly unfaithful to her husband—it may be that her sex is of strictly secondary importance. Delibes could also be attacking the mentality she personifies, a mentality that contemporary Spanish intellectuals seem generally to consider typical of the bourgeoisie, a conservative or reactionary fixation on status symbols, class distinctions, and privileges, almost total unreflectiveness, lack of insight and foresight, selfishness, materialism, hypocrisy, false or purely negative virtues, intolerance, insincerity, and self-deception. Certainly this attitude is one aspect of the novel; not too obvious on first reading, it becomes apparent upon reexamination. If criticism of this mental set was his principal intent, Delibes' choice of a woman to incarnate these principles could be explained as less likely to receive adverse political interpretations.

The novel achieves other ends which could also justify its composition. It is a study of marriage and marital misunderstanding, of a near-total diversity of interests, and incompatibility of personalities. This is what eventually destroys Mario, regardless of the official cause of his death. Such mismating is serious in Spain, where divorce is still not recognized, and while it is unlikely that Delibes intended to make a case for divorce, he has nonetheless shown how much destruction of human potential, frustration, and misery can result from prolonging such a relationship for a lifetime. It is also significant that Mario (representing social reform) is misunderstood, ridiculed, and seldom taken seriously by his wife (or by the bourgeois mentality). In the same way that other authors have employed the Cain and Abel motif to symbolize Spanish internal strife, Delibes could have chosen the marital relationship, for between the two, Carmen and Mario embody many attitudes which came into conflict in the Civil War. It can be deduced that Mario's family was Republican (his brothers were imprisoned during the war), while Carmen's family clearly belonged to the Nationalists, and her father was a rabid Monarchist. Carmen herself admires the monarchy largely for its pomp and ceremony.

The novel has twenty-eight divisions, an unnumbered section at the beginning which sets the scene for Carmen's last night with Mario, then twenty-six numbered chapters, each beginning with a passage from the Bible, and a final unnumbered section which takes place the following morning. In the first division, which functions as something of a prologue, the reader learns of Mario's death; at the end of a long day beginning with her discovery of her husband dead in bed, Carmen has just closed the door after the final visitor. Sensations of the day are presented in a jumbled montage of disconnected dialogue and impressions, showing Carmen's lack of authenticity, the childish egotism which actually made her resent the final courtesies paid her husband. She wished to be the protagonist of these scenes, even to be the one receiving the obituary publicity (she almost gave her own name to the newspaper). Delibes emphasizes by certain actions and phrases her concern with her appearance. Carmen is dressed in a black sweater which she knows is indecently tight for the occasion, but she is proud of her bust and does not change. As Mario's death brings important men whom she would have liked to entertain, she tries to take advantage of their visits for social purposes. Carmen is not the only hypocrite in this gathering; several incidents show that many are there only out of a sense of obligation. The insignificance of Mario's death for them is seen in banal conversations and occasional criticism of his "revolutionary" views. Those who seem most sincerely affected are people from the lower class, many of whom he had helped.

Delibes conveys a strong sense of artificiality in the fixed phrases, the set condolences, the interminable repetition of a few stock sentences: "Who would have believed it—such a young man!" "The heart is very treacherous, you know." "Take care of yourself, Carmen; the children need you." "He hasn't changed a bit, isn't even pale." "Resignation . . ." Interspersed are Carmen's automatic thanks for the visits, awkward silences, moments when someone says the wrong thing or tells an out-of-place joke to dispel the tension. Social implications are transmitted in the difficult moments resulting when members of the proletariat make comments which the bourgeoisie prefers not to understand, or when Carmen attempts to relegate those of the lower class to the kitchen, separating them from the visitors she wishes to impress.

It is nearly midnight when the last visitor leaves, and Carmen, alone with the body at her own request, takes Mario's Bible, with his favorite passages marked, and sits down near him to read. Each of the following twenty-six chapters is written as a single long paragraph, beginning with a biblical citation, often left incomplete when Carmen relates the idea with some previous disagreement with Mario and commences a tangential discourse and free association. This is often ironic, for the reader is aware that Carmen misinterprets the intent of many of the passages, giving them a meaning suited to her own interests, while her memory of Mario's acts shows that he not only understood but lived in accord with these verses. This Carmen is unable to perceive.

Carmen is not entirely to blame for her obtuseness and frivolity. Her memories make it clear that she is a product of her upbringing (and this is a generic trait). Her mother imbued her with her own prejudices, desire for status, and stereotyped ideas of women's duties and privileges. She had no appreciation or understanding of the books Mario wrote, partly because she is not too intelligent, but also because her mother ridiculed books, saying that they were useful only to carry on the head for posture practice. While all the evidence indicates that Mario was a model of marital fidelity, patience, and husbandly virtues, Carmen (perhaps reacting to the masculine stereotype) insists upon finding reasons for doubting him. From the grief of Encarna, widow of Mario's brother, she gathers fuel for her suspicion that an adulterous relationship existed between them. Her insistent wish to believe him unfaithful receives another explanation when it becomes clear that she herself has been extremely indiscreet, and while she denies having been physically unfaithful, her self-deception is such that the reader is left wondering. If she did not commit adultery, it was not due to her refusal but because Paco, a now-wealthy former beau, restrained himself. Carmen believes herself to be the perfect wife and mother (she has totally absorbed the Spanish idealization of her role), and it would be extremely difficult for her to admit her own infidelity even to herself. Thus she also insists on doubting Mario's statement made to her years before, that he was "as virgin as she" at marriage, although he did not consider this a virtue but the result of timidity. It is necessary for her to feel that he has consistently lied to her, that she has not been the only woman in his life. Apparently there were many arguments about this over the years.

Another principal area of dispute was socio-economic. Carmen wanted Mario to make more money, and believed that he had had various chances to do so, such as writing the books she wanted him to (third-rate novels) rather than his theoretical and philosophical works. She wanted a car, which he refused to buy. It is abundantly clear that for her it is primarily a status symbol, desired because all her friends have one, and she is mortified because "in his position" Mario insists upon riding a bicycle. Carmen wanted more servants, recalling her pampered childhood, and feels humiliated because she has only one maid. She reflects that it is better that her mother died before seeing her in such straits. For her, it is an indication that times are bad because servants now earn more, and not (as Mario said) a sign of progress. The good times were when servants received only room and board, and her father remains a generous figure in her mind because he used to say to leave a bite for the kitchen help.

Mario was an inner-directed person; Carmen is almost totally other-directed. She lives for the Thursday afternoon teas with her friends, and her greatest satisfactions come from their approval. She is constantly preoccupied with public opinion, "what people will say," most particularly the opinions of the handful of middle-aged women who are her closest associates. Delibes reveals the shallowness of these relationships, the backbiting and secret scorns, and the fact that none of them really knows each other, nor do they wish to penetrate beneath the facade. The superficial plane is more secure and comfortable. Obviously much the same was true of Carmen's marriage, though Mario tried to communicate with her in vain, resigning himself to intimate solitude after years of frustration. The only one to understand him among Carmen's friends is Ester, who reads and admires his books, a fact that Carmen resents and ridicules. She is horrified that young Mario, the eldest son, so resembles his father, and mentally swears to dominate and change him.

Carmen learned from her brother-in-law that Mario secretly wrote poetry, much of it dedicated to her, which flattered her vanity, but when he refused to show her these verses, she concluded that he must have been thinking of another woman. Now a woman of forty, Carmen is bulging and fading, but (she insists) still good-looking. One of her intimate satisfactions comes from the fact that a neighborhood grocer never fails to express a rather vulgar admiration when she passes in her tight sweater. She repeatedly reiterates that she pays no attention, but clearly remembers every word. Part of her inner contradiction results from the conflict between her need for masculine admiration, physically expressed, and the education she received, defining the feminine role as modest, essentially passive, prudent, and horrified by sex. Although the solemnity of the moment should preclude such thoughts, much of her mental activity during the "five hours with Mario" revolves around other men who have made advances to her. She affirms that she is disgusted, but it is clear that she does so only because she believes this to be the reaction of any "decent" woman. With her actions and dress she provokes and invites further masculine advances.

Carmen's insensitivity is clearly revealed in her recollections of the Civil War. The times spent in the bomb shelters were extremely amusing for her, and she rather sadistically enjoyed the fear and humiliation of the losers. As her family was well-situated, she recalls as one of the major privations having foregone dessert one day a week, with candy as a substitute. On the other hand, she is totally without sympathy for those who died, immune to the suffering that she witnessed, particularly when it involved the lower class, even though many such people were fighting for "her" cause. Her contribution to the war effort consisted of being a pen pal for a poorly educated soldier, but this ended abruptly when once he asked her to go out with him, as "common soldiers are low-class people."

Carmen's ethics are also extremly personal and relative. She does not understand and even disapproves of Mario's integrity, his refusal to play the "influence" game, and considers him impractical, stubborn, and stupid. But the moral or sexual misconduct she censures in others always finds some excuse if it happens in her family. This is summarized by young Mario in a discussion the following morning when he asks his mother, "Has it ever seemed suspicious to you that the concept of right and justice should always coincide exactly with our interests?" As the reader learns, Carmen wavers in that conviction only once, and this constitutes her true motive for spending these last hours alone with Mario. For some time (perhaps weeks or a few months) she has been seeing a former friend, Paco Alvarez, usually on seemingly accidental occasions, as he would give her a ride when she was walking or waiting for a bus. She finds him attractive, but it is obvious that an even greater attraction is his financial success and expensive, flashy car. As she insists in her attempted self-vindication, she felt hypnotized in his presence. She is nearly paralyzed as well, for she offers no resistance, despite awareness that she should, when he begins to make advances. Without admitting it, Carmen obviously realizes that she is morally guilty, for if the affair was not consummated, it was because Paco changed his mind at the last moment. Carmen's lack of sincerity is so great that she cannot even be honest with herself, but at the same time she is unable to quiet a feeling of guilt, and as a consequence desperately attempts to use Mario to soothe her conscience.

There is a doubt insinuated as to the cause of Mario's death. The doctor, a family friend, apparently certifies that it was a heart attack, but no autopsy is done, and he observes that heart problems are rare in asthenics. The possibility of suicide is implied, and this, combined with Carmen's guilty conscience, apparently suggests to her that Mario could somehow have learned of her indiscretion and killed himself. Carmen never actually voices that fear, but her sense of guilt grows through the night, and her defenses against facing her responsibility begin to crumble. At last she has no rationalizations and excuses left, and is overpowered by the imperious necessity of receiving his forgiveness before it is forever too late. She demands a reply to her "confession," insulting her dead husband for his impassiveness and failure to respond to her pleas with some sign that he understands. At some point she begins to rave and is heard by young Mario. Carmen has only one moment of real sincerity and authenticity in the novel, and perhaps in her life, when she cries to the body: "Look at me, Mario! I have nothing to be ashamed of, Mario, I swear it! Look at me a moment, just a second, listen to me, don't pretend you don't hear, Mario, I beg you, I haven't done anything wrong, I swear it! May I die if it isn't true! But don't shrug your shoulders, please, look at me, I beg you on my knees, I can't stand it, Mario, I swear it, look at me or I'll go crazy, please!"[4]

When young Mario enters, the spell is broken; her one moment of unfeigned emotion has passed, and Carmen returns to her automatic, conventional patterns, the meaningless words of endearment constantly on her lips, the proper formulas, the socially right behavior. This is the principal function of the book's final section, something of an epilogue, for it shows that the crisis has passed, and Carmen returns to "normal," somewhat older, perhaps, but essentially unchanged. What a lifetime with Mario has not achieved, this "moment of truth" will not accomplish, either. On a socio-political plane, the novel lends itself to allegorical interpretation. Perhaps it is better, however, to leave it with the possibilities indicated, but choosing none of them here. It would be feasible, based on acquaintance with Delibes' social thought, to decide with reasonable certainty that his purpose was to denounce the social effects and implications of the bourgeois mentality, but this also limits the novel. It has other meanings which the novelist may not have foreseen.

CHAPTER 12

Society versus the Individual

CONCERN with the problematic nature of the individual's relationship to society is present in one form or another in Delibes' novels from the first to the most recent, sometimes only implicit, but often as a major theme. The novelist's general attitude seems to have changed from an initial relative optimism to progressively greater pessimism or fear. In *The Cypress*, Pedro represents an affirmation of individual principles and rights, even to extremes of isolationism, an exaggerated egotism which the narrator does not support, but seemingly understands. Sebastián in *Still It Is Day* struggles with the conflict between his own rights and needs and the necessities of others, arriving at some sort of synthesis whereby he satisfies himself through service to those around him. In *The Path*, Daniel suffers from the divergence between his own desires and the demands and expectations of society (education, material success) as represented by his father. Cecilio Rubes *(My Adored Son Sisí)*, another extreme egotist, is utterly lacking in civic conscience or sense of responsibility to community and nation. His first impulse after the outbreak of the Civil War is to flee to Portugal and let the others fight it out.

The problem is essentially that broached in the truncated, posthumous work of the philosopher Ortega, *El hombre y la gente (Man and People)*, and the underlying concern in each case is basically ethical. While less evident in the *Diaries* of Lorenzo (partly due to the nature of the narrative consciousness), the same problem area is suggested by his concern with the observance of game laws in the common interest, his counterbalancing sense of pleasure upon escaping from society to the solitude of the hunt, as well as an occasionally acute awareness of the limitations imposed by his relative social rank. The emphasis is shifted in *The Red Leaf* from the individual's relationship to society to underscoring society's responsibility to individuals, specifically the aged and underprivileged. *The Rats* presents a clash between primitive individualism and a more modern, although backward and defective society. The individual is destroyed, not by society alone but by the forces of nature, and the character of tío Ratero himself, all contributing to his downfall. In *Five Hours with Mario,* one principal cause for dispute between Carmen and her husband was the issue of social responsibility. Carmen is incapable of real altruism, and her interest in others is conditioned exclusively by their reflections upon herself: What will society (the upper class) think of her? Mario in some respects may be an alter ego of Delibes, a strong social conscience, relatively impervious to public opinion, who devotes a good deal of time and energy to bettering the lot of the proletariat, at least in the measure of one man's capacity.

I Parábola del náufrago (Parable of the Drowning Man)[1]

This book represents the total crushing of the individual by the collectivity, dehumanization and the loss of liberty as a result of the progressive encroachment by the state upon areas of the personal conscience and beliefs. Two symbolically dehumanized individuals undergo physical metamorphoses (representing spiritual degradation) as a result of punishment received for daring to question the omniscience of an all-powerful bureaucratic organization. This first appears to be economic in nature, but later proves more complex, probably representing the totalitarian state.

In the opening pages, Genaro, a friend of the protagonist, has been "demoted" for the offense of putting personal concerns before the interests of the organization and, chained nude in a doghouse and treated like a hound, has eventually acquired many canine habits and physical characteristics. A pariah because of his sin, "Gen" is avoided by all but Jacinto, prancing around puppy-like while the latter scratches him on the head. Gen gulps down morsels unchewed, laps up water, and when Jacinto eventually tires of his antics, lies down obediently. Only after several pages does Delibes begin to hint that Gen is not actually a large dog, or at least has not always been in his present form.

Gen's history is revealed in fragments, by means of Jacinto's thoughts, mostly interior monologue, occasionally a sort of dialogue with himself. He rationalizes that Gen is happier this way and has lost nothing important as his wife comes daily to walk him and his children play with him. After all, thinks Jacinto, "two feet or four, what difference does it make?" While he initially appears to accept Gen's punishment as wise and just, its unusual nature so bothers him that he is forced continually to attempt to justify it. During the course of the novel, Gen's fate increasingly obsesses Jacinto, combining with the menace to his own personality and subtly foreshadowing Jacinto's eventual downfall. The final metamorphosis of the protagonist into a sheep is handled in slow, indirect fashion, emphasizing his vague sensations of the physical changes undergone, so that only when the transformation is complete is its nature clear. Gen's "demotion" seems directly related to "thought crimes," and Jacinto reflects almost at the outset that "all evils come from that [i.e., thinking]and after all, if thinking is what makes us suffer, why the devil do we think?" (pp. 16–17). A phrase repeated in a variety of situations is that "The bad thing is not the fly; it is thinking about [i.e., awareness of] the fly." In other words, an ill is not an ill while one is not conscious of it. But despite these mental self-admonitions, Jacinto is unable to refrain from thinking, or to channel his confused, chaotic thoughts into the socially acceptable patterns, and this dooms him.

The principle of metamorphosis, the nightmarish and delirious atmosphere, a mixture of reality and the possible fantastic, as well as the nature of the mysterious bureaucracy and the utter solitude of the protagonist, all suggest Kafka. Some readers might think of other potential sources, particularly Ionesco's *Rhinoceros,* with the similar principle of metamorphosis. The association would not be entirely inappropriate, for Ionesco shares with Kafka the sentiment of cruelty and absurdity of existence, and both writers have additional points of contact with Delibes' latest novel in their expression of the fear, anguish, and threats to liberty of the too-orderly chaos in which we live. However, Delibes has not read widely in the theater, and if he had a specific inspiration for *Parable,* it is more likely to have come from the Czech novelist. Delibes had read works of Kafka some years before, to judge from passing references in lectures and interviews, but it is interesting that *Parable* appeared slightly over one year after Delibes' visit to Prague, a trip which probably coincided with the genesis of at least part of the novel.

The crushing of the Czech experiment in liberty by the Russian government could possibly be reflected in *Parable* by the annihilation of the only two individuals who dare, or simply chance, to be different. However, there is no revolt as such; neither character is an intellectual or hero, or even interested in politics, and any manifestations of deviance are simply instinctive evasive tactics by the personality sensing its danger, the imminence of absorption. There is no conscious aggression, only the increasingly frantic floundering of the drowning man (hence the title). Delibes does not give environmental details suggesting a specific foreign country; the scanty ambientation is Spanish, consisting of a few *costumbrista* touches, with much that is vague, stereotyped, or deliberately non-local. *Parable* could thus equally well be an indictment of the Spanish government, with its abrogation of individual liberties and rights, and its vast bureaucratic structure, conflicting with local traditions of exaggerated individualism and separatism. At the same time, much is applicable to any totalitarian organization, any oligarchy. The fact that the novelist gives no name to the city setting may be due to his wish not to attack the Spanish state directly, or equally well to a desire to generalize the implications of his *Parable,* pointing out universal dangers. The near anonymity of the setting, however, is significant; this is the first work of Delibes to lack sufficient realistic detail to permit its being assigned a fairly specific geographic location.

Much of the novel is written as a stream of consciousness, with extensive interior monologue. Delibes has pursued the direction of the technical innovations developed in *Five Hours with Mario,* advancing even farther in modifications of syntax, in stylistic change particularly suited to psychological probing and dissection, or exposition. *Parable* is frequently characterized by extremely long and complicated sentences, a confusing agglutination of cumulative phrases. The punctuation is deliberately arbitrary and capricious, at times almost nonexistent and at others excessive, so abundant as to interfere with the reader's comprehension. The protagonist, desperately attempting to salvage some shreds of personality, has invented an artificial language (actually characteristic of certain severe neuroses and psychoses). Part of this novel (which is dedicated to Jacinto) utilizes his language, one of whose characteristics is the foreshortening of words, perhaps reflecting the influence of abbreviations, common in today's nomenclature and advertising, or of telegraphy or shorthand, since the protagonist is obviously menaced, among other things, by those forms of progress which restrict or minimize individuality. Jacinto's "language" increases the stylistic and mental confusion by replacing conventional punctuation signs [e.g., *period* for the dot at the end of a sentence, *comma* instead of the usual symbol] with the word names. The appearance of many lengthy passages is an endless flow of words, a complete absence of punctuation, sometimes for a page or more. The following will serve as an example: "Behind the fence comma to the right of the iron gate comma next to the large conifer comma was the little house of Genaro open parenthesis who was now called Gen colon Here, Gen! close parenthesis comma like a doll's house comma also white comma the roof of grey slate and when it rained or Baudelio Villamayor the gardener . . . sprinkled comma the grey slate roof turned black and shining as if recently varnished period" (p. 10). As the ellipsis indicates, the example has been foreshortened, with the elimination of another long parenthetical explanation, but its inclusion would have added nothing essential to the illustration of the technique. The portions written in this fashion are usually expository in nature, so that even the supposedly objective narrative voice contributes to the hallucinatory atmosphere increasingly experienced and communicated by Jacinto via the interior monologues, written with conventional punctuation for the most part, although without quotation marks, which tend to be omitted throughout, compounding the difficulties of a complex, serialized syntax. The frequent enumerations, repetitions, interruptions, parenthetical explanations, and other fragmentations likewise call attention to the peculiar punctuation (or lack thereof). On other occasions, Delibes seems playfully to use a superabundance of punctuation marks, with commas between almost every syntactical unit, even between nouns and their adjectives, subject and verb, and before and after conjunctions. Verbs frequently come in series, adding to the impression of seriously jumbled mental processes.

Delibes' purpose is of course to enable readers to experience the confused and disoriented sensations of Jacinto, something of the "feel" of a personality in disintegration. The same devices underscore the artificiality of the setting and the thoroughly conventionalized, regimented existence, bereft of all naturalness and spontaneity. By such means, and especially in the language invented by Jacinto, Delibes achieves another purpose: the satire of certain modern literary theories involving the breakdown or destruction of the language. His attitude— especially relevant here—toward certain techniques of the antinovel has already been remarked.[2] As reported in *La estafeta literaria*,[3] a lecture by Delibes in the Ateneo in Madrid may further illustrate this aspect of *Parable*. Delibes felt harshly toward certain tendencies of the contemporary novel, especially what he considered excessive theorizing on the part of novelists: "We overload ourselves with theories and forget the practice." "Today our aesthetic ideas occupy more space than our works." He also criticized literary propagandizing and observed: "The novel is becoming nothing more than a technical experiment. There is no room for sentiment." Various formal characteristics of *Parable* can thus be partially explained as ironic reactions to contemporary experiments with structure, technique, and language.

In one of the few relevant criticisms to appear to date, quite a different evaluation is given. The novel is discussed in the context of other experiments by contemporary Spanish writers under the influence of the French "new novel," and seen as "a certain rupture on the part of the writer with his earlier work. It must be said that from this break, the novelist comes out as depersonalized as his protagonist. The subject, as well as the elements with which it is elaborated, give the impression of being dragged in from outside, instead of flowing . . . from original, internal creative necessity. . ."[4] This is to ignore completely the importance of the individual and the menace posed by mechanized society in Delibes' works during the entire course of his career, and to allow the superficial stylistic and technical differences to obscure the essential thematic similarities. Then, too, despite the changes in style and technique, there are (as will be seen) antecedents in previous writings, as well as other elements that are still sufficiently unchanged as to be very identifiably Delibes. It likewise seems inexact to say that Jacinto is "depersonalized" in the sense in which this critic means it, for while he may be robbed of the last shreds of humanity or individualism, he manages to achieve a haunting reality in his struggle to save his personality. The critic just cited continues: "And what of the supplanting of the author's own natural style by the discursive, zigzagging paragraphs which introduce in the novel that famous 'wordiness' which, as we have seen, is one of the distinctive characteristics of the *nouveau roman?*" There is no denying the "wordiness" of much of the novel, but it must be remembered that Delibes himself has more than one "natural style," as implied in this analysis. While it is a different "wordiness," excess verbosity is to be found in three of the four earliest novels, and a return to less "natural" or simple construction can be detected in the short stories written from 1963 on, a tendency more pronounced in *Five Hours with Mario*. This analysis overlooks definite similarities with that novel and the technically related short stories of recent vintage, particularly when speaking of "rupture," for the most that can be said is that there has been a further (and perhaps more pronounced or rapid) development in the direction of "wordiness." Neither does Corrales Egea take into account the pronouncements by Delibes which clearly suggest that *Parable* is more a satire of the *nouveau roman* than a simple imitation.

On the other hand, when one of Spain's better-informed contemporary critics associates this work with the French "new novel," having had prolonged close contact with the French literary scene, the possibility that Delibes is (at least to some extent) writing in that vein must be considered seriously. Perhaps, in the tradition of Cervantes, he has parodied a particular type of novel by producing an excellent example of that genre. What must be remembered, however, is his literary independence, his personal and novelistic individualism, and the refusal until now to follow literary fads. Combined with his criticisms of the "new novel," and his oft-reiterated preoccupation for the menace to the individual posed by contemporary society, it can only be concluded that if Delibes has appropriated certain techniques and characteristics of the *nouveau roman,* he has done so in the same spirit of satire and irony which typify so many of his other works, and not as a serious imitator of that school.

In the lecture by Delibes cited above, there is this statement: "A novel requires at least a man, a landscape and a passion. Without these, I believe, there is no novel." Perhaps because *Parable of the Drowning Man* is a work where the last two have disappeared and man in the real sense is in the process of vanishing, the author has qualified the work as a parable. He is not simply avoiding the categorizing of the work as a novel, however; it does have the moral and didactic qualities of the parable.

Jacinto is first revealed as lonely, with a solitude implicit in his affection for the dog-man, a relationship with no counterpart among his co-workers. Besides, Jacinto is an orphan, without family ties, his life almost entirely bounded by his employment. He is compulsive, overly exact in unimportant details, meticulous, insecure, with a great longing for affection, pallid, respectful and submissive, timid to a painful degree, but nonetheless a responsible functionary. He is employed as a calligrapher in the gigantic enterprise of "Don Abdón,"[5] omnipresent figure who seems to be not only head of state but a sort of god, who has all but totally absorbed private and public life, the economy, and religion. He resembles both Buddha and a hermaphrodite, and is called "the most motherly of fathers." Jacinto is indistinguishable from the mass: "neither tall nor short, nor fat nor thin . . . a man in a series," a production-line product, prototype of his culture and his epoch. Such an individual could hardly be expected to resist the onslaught of an all-encroaching society, yet even he, physically and psychologically weak, struggles for self-preservation.

As in his other works, Delibes in *Parable* employs much repetition and a good deal of exaggeration, tending to the caricaturesque. Figures are characterized largely by their manias or peculiarities, and most secondary characters are mere caricatures, one or two pathetic, but many grotesque. Jacinto begins as a caricature, more complex than the others (or at best a stereotype), but manages, in his desperate fight for survival, to become a memorable figure, suprisingly human in his dehumanization. The device of repetition serves to define limits, to indicate the trap in which Jacinto strains, and to reinforce the nightmarish atmosphere. Many incidents in *Parable* are comic without being really funny, incongruous, bizarre, and implicitly frightening, or inherently more deserving of compassion than laughter. There are echoes of *Brave New World* and *1984,* with many personages emerging as quasirobots or automatons. This is particularly noticeable in the scenes which take place in the establishment of Don Abdón, but also in relation to authority and its representatives.

Jacinto's occupation, like that of his two hundred co-workers in the same large room, has been made superfluous by technology, for he is merely doing the work of an adding machine, or else carefully writing ciphers. He has not the slightest idea of what, if anything, is represented by the numbers, and it is forbidden to ask. To all intents and purposes, these are human machines, synchronized by Darío Esteban, a Gestapo-like foreman who indicates when to sit and when to rise, who scrutinizes their movements, productivity, and expressions, and seemingly functions as a "thought policeman." In this paternalistic, totalitarian system, the employees are treated like schoolchildren, scolded, punished by kneeling in a corner during "recess," or forced to write one thousand times, "I will be diligent." The nature of Don Abdón's business remains as much a mystery to the reader as to Jacinto, but it emerges as all-engulfing. The interior of the office building resembles a combination of a mosque, a tabernacle, and a Baroque church in the worst of garish tastes, while the working atmosphere is cultlike, a religion of commerce. The foreman maintains his inscrutable vigilance from a minaret, and the mysterious private office where Don Abdón is enthroned on a sort of altar is like the holy of holies, accessible only to the "high priest," Darío Esteban. Following his baton, the calligraphers chant in unison slogans such as "Adding is the most noble activity of man on the face of the earth"; "Talking about sports [and implicitly politics] is even more healthy than practicing them"; "Order is liberty"; and "The avoidance of responsibility is the first step to happiness."

While much of the novel consists of anecdotes of a *costumbrista* nature, actually unrelated to the narrative and serving only as background (or possibly to distract the censor), there is a plot line, although not easily unraveled because of the way time is handled. The interior monologue of Jacinto is simultaneously retrospective and present, mixing fantasy, hallucination, and fact, and it is no simple task to separate these and establish sequences. The essential action begins when Jacinto swoons during work, dizzied by writing zeros and apparently tormented by the desire to learn what his sums represent. He is summoned to the office of Don Abdón, where a cryptic sentence is pronounced: "The hedge is the refuge of the timid." Jacinto is transported to a remote cabin retreat and instructed to sow a bag of seeds, which he does dutifully. Within hours, they have sprouted, and soon a wall of plants growing like Jack's famous beanstalk isolates Jacinto from the world. The barrier becomes increasingly monstrous and voracious, devouring the intervening land and threatening the cabin. Jacinto, initially intrigued, becomes frantic at the prospect of absorption by this vegetable Hydra, and tries a variety of means of escape. Interwoven with his ever more frantic efforts to penetrate the living barricade are a montage of confused memories, incidents revealing the mental state which led to his "sin" and punishment.

Perhaps the most important motif, aside from the nature of the society itself, is the grotesque death of the dog-man, Genaro. He literally "died like a dog," killed by a gardener while pursuing a female cocker, with the gardener's rationalization that he appeared mad. He is decapitated and an autopsy performed (as with rabid dogs), after which dehumanization is carried to its ultimate extreme, beyond death, when the demand is made of his widow to relinquish human burial. The medical examiner is intrigued with his unique specimen, and his offer of reimbursement is reinforced by the state's offer to guarantee an income if she acceeds. Her agreement not to insist on Christian last rites symbolizes the loss of Genaro's soul, the one remaining vestige of humanity, annihilated by Don Abdón.

Jacinto, initially confident in his battle with the engulfing thicket, attempts to cut a path through the plant wall. Frustrated and exhausted by the miniature jungle which grows faster than he can work, he attempts to tunnel underneath, but is nearly trapped in the pit by encroaching roots and creepers. Becoming frantic, he begins to remove the cabin's fuel supply, drenching an area with gasoline and setting it aflame. When the conflagration dies, he finds that it has burned only a fraction of the way through the hedge. A homemade bomb also fails. Finally he demolishes all the furniture, the shutters, and heaps everything combustible, including the food, next to the menacing foliage, but this fire is likewise inadequate. Almost crazed by fear, he attempts to send word of his predicament to the outside world, a situation fraught with existentialist implications, and powerfully symbolic of his isolation and solitude. Catching wild birds, he attaches his cry for help to over a hundred of them, but despairs the next day upon finding them all roosting in the thicket, which continues its visible and audible expansion.

A plane carrying Darío Esteban flies over the cabin, and Jacinto catches a glimpse of his mocking face, but fails to suspect even then that his torture could be premeditated. Believing himself to be saved, he collapses in the cabin, physically and emotionally extenuated. During an indefinite period of time, he sleeps, awaking only intermittently to eat. He notices that the plants, once so threatening, begin to exercise a strange attraction, and nibbles tendrils penetrating the wall. Later, he feels an irresistible desire to gambol on all fours, and still later perceives light wool covering his body. When a team equipped with flame-throwers finally cuts through the wall of vegetation, the metamorphosis is complete. Jacinto is able to perceive their excuses—"Who could have imagined that that hybrid would be so vigorous?"—but is unable to respond with more than "Baaa!" A medical examination results in the verdict that the subject is a fine ram, suitable for breeding stock.

During his most intense fear and panic, Jacinto imagines the plight of a sailor, trapped in a sunken ship slowly filling with water. Knowing that he is doomed, he nevertheless clings desperately to life, continuing to swim as water fills the cabin, holding his face above the rising water, avidly swallowing the last gulps of air. This "parable" of the fight for survival, the instinct of self-preservation functioning in even the most hopeless situation, clearly applies to Jacinto, whose physical survival is purchased at the cost of his human condition. While Don Abdón, especially in his farcical public appearances, bears a marked resemblance to Francisco Franco, the organization itself, whether religious, commercial, or political, has no specific ideologies. The slogans are totalitarian or paternalistic, but could equally well be Fascist or Marxist. Some aspects of the novel might be seen as a more generalized attack on contemporary civilization, but this is of secondary importance. Like Ortega in *The Revolt of the Masses,* Delibes is concerned not merely with the physical survival or comfort of the individual, but with the mass psychology and the quality of life in our times. His *Parable* is a lesson, a warning, and perhaps a cry for help, help in saving that which is most human in humanity.

CHAPTER 13

Summary and Conclusions

DELIBES is almost universally accepted as one of the most significant contemporary Spanish novelists. Together with Camilo José Cela and Ana María Matute, he occupies the forefront among living writers in his country, and is known abroad in translations to Portuguese, English, German, Swedish, Italian, French, and other languages. In addition to his professional teaching duties and his distinguished novelistic career, he rose to be one of Spain's leading newspapermen, and in that capacity attracted notice and opposition as an outspoken critic of his government's social, agricultural, and economic policies.

From conservative beginnings within the realistic movement, Delibes has evolved as a narrator, incorporating in his literary repertoire many of this century's important technical and structural innovations. His style, initially florid and overly ample, was progressively pruned and polished, becoming more direct, conversational, and precise. Most recently, his latest works show a return to a more complex syntax, but it is of a different nature than in the early novels, and the intent has changed. Delibes now integrates form with content, and the new convolutions of his prose reflect the troubled psychological atmosphere and torment of his characters. The early novels showed an interest in psychological probing which began to diminish with *The Path*, resulting in more superficial, less individualized portrayals, almost without analysis, or with a generic or collective protagonist, as in the two *Diaries* and the work on rural Castile. In *Five Hours with Mario* and *Parable of the Drowning Man*, Delibes returns to in-depth psychological studies, albeit somewhat archetypical, of the middle-class housewife and the timid functionary. There has been a similar circular progression in thematics, in general terms, from concentration on the problems of individuals to social concerns, and back to the peril of the individual. This is reflected in the change from individual protagonist to double (in

The Red Leaf) and collective (in *The Path, The Rats)* and back to the single protagonist in the latest works. Symbolism, fairly evident in the early novels, almost disappears in the intermediate stage, becoming important again with *The Red Leaf* and in most narratives thereafter.

The most characteristic notes of Delibes' mature writing are his use of nicknames and tag lines, repetition, caricature, and portrayal through manias and quirks. Particularly striking is his frequent use of the abnormal or subnormal mentality, the primitive or elemental character, and the hunter. He frequently utilizes the technique of perspective or point of view, situating the reader within the consciousness or perceptions of the primitive (or otherwise abnormal) mentality. Also characteristic of most of the works composed after *The Path* is a peculiar, personal brand of humor, a mixture of understatement and exaggeration, ranging in intensity from light, almost imperceptible irony, to sarcasm, exacerbation, and the grotesque.

Themes preferably treated by Delibes include those concerning childhood and adolescence, old age, death, nature and the hunt, social inequities and economic problems, the plight of rural Castile, the city-country dichotomy, the problem of emigration, internal and external, the individual in his relation to others, the menace of mechanization and of other aspects of contemporary civilization, the dangers inherent in the society of masses, the difficulties of communication, the need for (and lack of) human warmth, the isolation and solitude of man in the twentieth century.

Seen in the total context of his novels, shorter fiction, works on travel and hunting, and his varied articles and lectures, Delibes emerges as a more complex writer than he appears at first glance to be. At least twice in his novelistic career, he has surprised critics who believed they had him pigeonholed, turning to styles and techniques so different that superficially they seemed to represent a complete break with former production. This was the case with the publication of *The Path,* whose style and thematics scarcely resembled those of the more ponderous and self-conscious first novels. With his last works, *Five Hours with Mario* and *Parable of a Drowning Man* (and most particularly the latter), the phenomenon has been repeated. Examination reveals, however, that these differences are not so complete as imagined by some. Throughout his career, Delibes has experimented with varying narrative techniques, and the impression of change is produced when a more or less startling technical innovation coincides with stylistic modifications. Thematically, his work has remained more constant.

Many motifs are present throughout: the obsessive shadow of death, the importance of nature (whether as a refuge or an additional hardship in a difficult existence), the preference for juvenile or elemental figures, the focus on Castile, the emphasis on economic factors, frequent pessimism and irony, and a constant implicit or explicit ethical orientation. While to date it would seem that the "essential" or most "typical" Delibes is found in the works between *The Path* and *Old Tales of Old Castile* (and this corresponds to generally held opinions), the novelist is still young and productive, and his latest works demonstrate conclusively the existence of a vigorous creative potential still untapped.

At present, Delibes' greatest importance would appear to be as the novelist of rural Castile, as an artist who has forcefully and knowledge-ably presented both the beauty and the tragedy of its soil and its people, infusing with humble but intense human drama a landscape once appreciated only aesthetically. While not ascribing to most of the tenets of the movement, Delibes is a significant social novelist, with a sincere but undogmatic concern for righting injustices and promoting reforms which will enable all Spaniards to enjoy basic human rights and comforts. His contributions in this area, totally lacking in the propaganda or ideological commitments of most other social novelists, are epitomized in *The Red Leaf, The Rats,* and *Old Tales of Old Castile,* although strong echoes are heard in *Five Hours with Mario.* The "concern for the Other" which the novelist stated inspired these works is rivalled only by Delibes' concern for the individual, also found in some of the novels just mentioned, and of an intensity qualifying this novelist to be cited together with Ortega for sounding the alarm of the threat posed to authentic personal existence by the society of masses, mass culture, and technological civilization. It is too soon to say that other elements may not subsequently preempt first place in Delibes' future writing, but these will certainly remain among his most significant and characteristic themes.

Delibes is a consistent writer, despite his evolution, with many constants and repetitions, and should his emphasis shift, it will almost certainly be to themes and techniques already foreshadowed in his published works. Despite his development and sustained artistic progress, there have been relatively few thematic changes. The social preoccupations, not really perceptible in his first novel (except in a negative sense) were already present in the second, and with the completion of *Still It Is Day,* the seeds of his constant themes had been sown almost totally, for they can be found in varying degrees and in different forms in the first two novels alone. There have subsequently been changes in emphasis and in the form of presentation, but Delibes' essential concerns today have long-standing literary antecedents in his work, usually reaching back to the first three of four years of his novelistic career.

In the opinion of a majority of critics, *The Path* and *The Rats* continue to be the preferred works by Delibes. While *The Path* is delightful, it does not seem to have the significance of *The Red Leaf, The Rats, Five Hours with Mario,* and *Parable of the Drowning Man,* all novels of a greater intensity and historical relevance, and of a comparable level of artistic perfection. Many critics also consider *Diary of a Hunter* a masterpiece, and it is certainly unrivalled in Spanish literature both with respect to language and mastery of the character portrayed. Thus, before reaching the age of fifty, Delibes has produced at least half a dozen novels worthy to be counted among the best of this century, several of them with excellent chances of outlasting the present era and enduring among the classics of the language. The novelist is now at the height of his creative powers, and can yet reasonably be expected to surpass these successes in the years to come.

Notes and References

Chapter One

1. This is the title of the translation by John and Brita Haycraft (New York: John Day Co., 1961).

2. Gonzalo Torrente Ballester, *Panorama de la literatura española contemporánea* (Madrid: Guadarrama [2 ed.,] 1962), pp. 426–27.

3. This fact is mentioned by Maximino Alvarez, "Vida y obra de Delibes," doctoral thesis, University of Salamanca, 1964, one of the principal sources of biographical material, together with the work of Hickey, cited below, and various autobiographical declarations and notes by Delibes himself, especially in the prologues to the three published volumes of his *Obra completa* (hereinafter called the *Complete Works;* see Bibliography).

4. *Complete Works*, Vol. II, 11.

5. Francisco de Mellado, *Guía*, "Origen de Valladolid," cited in Angel Lacalle, *Perfiles de España* (Barcelona: Bosch, 1948), p. 56.

6. Alvarez, p. 10.

7. Alvarez cites 1941 as the date for this employment, while Leo Hickey, *Cinco horas con Miguel Delibes* (Madrid: Editorial Prensa Española, 1968), gives 1942. There are certain other discrepancies, but Hickey seems to have relied heavily on Alvarez. However, his work is later, so that some differences could reflect rectifications by Delibes, whom Hickey interviewed at some length.

8. This is found in many interviews and autobiographical notes; translation here, as from all Spanish sources cited, is mine. Existing translations of works of Delibes have been consulted primarily for their introductions, independent of the language to which his books are translated, and except for their duly credited critical observations, translations have not been used.

9. The Spanish title is "Causas de disolución de las compañías anónimas," but the literal "anonymous companies" fails to convey the notion of a particular legal entity.

10. Interview by the present author with Delibes, Valladolid, February, 1966.

11. Rafael Vázquez-Zamora, "Miguel Delibes," in *Destino* (Barcelona), February 24, 1951, No. 707.

12, This is the date given by Hickey; Alvarez states that it was a year earlier.

13. Francisco Alvaro, "Conversación y semblanza de Miguel Delibes," *ABC* (Madrid), May 10, 1958.

14. Hickey, p. 24.

15. Lecture by Delibes in the Ateneo of Madrid, May 5, 1965.

16. One of the most distasteful was by Pedro de Lorenzo, "A la sombra de un fallo literario," in the Falangist daily, *Arriba* (Madrid), attacking not only Delibes but all who had commented favorably upon his novel.

17. M. R. Villén, "Entrevista con Miguel Delibes," *Teleradio* (Madrid), October 22, 1962.

18. "Noticia de Miguel Delibes," *Libros y discos,* No. 2, September, 1962), p. 5.

19. Interview by the present author, Valladolid, February, 1966.

20. *Vivir al día* (Barcelona: Destino, 1968), p. 7.

21. *La primavera de Praga* (Madrid: Alianza Editorial, 1968), p. 11.

22. *Ibid.,* p. 9.

23. This information comes from a letter written by Delibes to the present author, September 8, 1970. The anthology itself has not been examined for this study.

24. José Corrales Egea, "Situación actual de la novela española: La 'contraola'," *Insula,* No. 282 (Supplement), May, 1970, pp. 21–24.

25. In the letter cited in note 23, the novelist expresses some doubt that this novel will ever be published.

Chapter Two

1. Barcelona: Destino, 1963. References to the first novel will use for convenience an abbreviated title, *The Cypress.*

2. M. García Viñó, *Novela española actual* (Madrid: Guadarrama, 1967), "Miguel Delibes: Entre la primera y la segunda naturaleza," p. 43.

3. Manuel del Arco, "Mano a mano," *La vanguardia* (Barcelona), May 15, 1963.

4. A. Iglesias Laguna, *Treinta años de novela española, 1938–1968* (Madrid: Editorial "Prensa Española," 1969), p. 274.

5. A literary movement imported to Spain from Latin America, primarily in poetry, characterized by a preoccupation with the beautiful and esoteric expression.

6. Leo Hickey, *Cinco horas con Miguel Delibes* (Madrid: Editorial "Prensa Española," 1968), p. 110.

7. Juan Luis Alborg, *Hora actual de la novela española* (Madrid: Taurus, 1958), I, 154.

8. Barcelona: Destino, 1949. Consulted for this study is the second edition, 1962, p. 9.

9. Barcelona: Destino, 1968.

10. *Op. cit.,* pp. 7–8.

11. Hickey, who includes a survey of the priests created by Delibes, notes that this friar is one of only two clerics in the novelist's work who are not parish priests, and that only Padre Matías seems to be a sound theologian.

12. *Op. cit.,* pp. 115–16.

Chapter Three

1. Among these are such reputable critics as José Luis Cano, who concluded his review for *Insula* (March, 1951) with the statement that "God had marked the path for 'el Mochuelo,' and his path was in the village."

2. M. García Viño, *Novela española actual* (Madrid: Guadarrama, 1967), p. 35.

3. G. Torrente Ballester, *Panorama de la literatura española contemporánea* (Madrid: Guadarrama [2 ed.,] pp. 426–27.

4. Barcelona: Destino. Volume I, 1963; Volume II, 1966.

5. This was part of a critique by Guillermo Díaz-Plaja, broadcast on January 23, 1951.

6. José María P. Lozano, in an article in *Signo* dated February 12, 1951, recognized that *El camino* represented a technical advance over previous works, and even called it one of the best products of contemporary Spanish literature, but nonetheless stated that it was morally dangerous.

7. Interview published in *Región* (Oviedo), April 26, 1964.

8. García Viño, p. 23.

9. García Viño, p. 31. This critic alleges that in the novels after *El camino,* reality itself becomes a caricature, and that beneath this lies "an almost total scorn of the author for his characters or what they represent."

10. Leo Hickey, *Cinco horas con Miguel Delibes* (Madrid: Editorial "Prensa Española," 1968), p. 91.

11. *El camino,* edition by José Amor Vázquez and Ruth Kossoff (New York: Holt, 1960), p. vi.

12. This is perhaps Delibes' most widely diffused work, and one almost alone in having had a study in English devoted solely to it. (E. A. Johnson, Jr., "Miguel Delibes, *El camino*—A Way of Life," *Hispania,* XLVI, No. 4 [December, 1963,] 748–752.

Chapter Four

1. Barcolona: Destino, 1953. Perhaps the most literal translation is "My Idolized Son," which does convey the idea of sin (idolatry) the

novelist may have wished to suggest, but "adored" seems a more accurate description of the father's attitude.

2. Interview with the present author, Valladolid, February, 1966.

3. Manuel G. Cerezales, *"Mi idolatrado hijo Sisí,"* in *Informaciones* (Madrid), October 29, 1953, p. 11. This evaluation so stung Delibes that he replied in a public lecture a few months later, defending his moral intent.

4. Leo Hickey, *Cinco horas con Miguel Delibes* (Madrid: Editorial "Prensa Española," 1968), p. 116.

5. Delibes, "Autocrítica de *Mi idolatrado hijo Sisí*," lecture in the Ateneo of Madrid, April, 1954.

6. Hickey, pp. 270–71.

7. Pablo Gil Casado, *La novela social española* (Barcelona: Seix Barral, 1968), p. 20. This is the only work of Delibes discussed by Casado, who excludes the others as not conforming to his criteria for the *novela social*.

8. Phillip Pollack, Introduction to British edition of *El camino* (London: Harrap, 1963), pp. 15–16.

9. The greatest similarity is in the use of newspaper headlines, articles, advertisements, and similar other documents of the time. Various Spanish critics mentioned the probable influence of Dos Passos' *USA* trilogy, and particularly of *Manhattan Transfer*, but as was the case with alleged resemblances between his first two novels and well-known foreign works, Delibes reiterated his ignorance of the supposed models. In this case, especially, it seems logical that his association with *El norte de Castilla* and access to its archives might have produced the coincidence without any direct technical influence.

Chapter Five

1. Interview with the present author, Valladolid, February, 1966. In his prologue to *La mortaja,* a collection of short stories published by Delibes after initial completion of the present study, Miguel Angel Pastor makes a similar affirmation and develops some of the correspondences between short story and novel discussed in this chapter (Madrid: Alianza Editorial, 1970, pp. 7–31.

2. Barcelona: Caralt, 1954.

3. *Mundo hispánico,* Año II, No. 21 (December, 1949), pp. 58–59.

4. *Mundo hispánico,* Año XVI, No. 182 (May, 1963), pp. 73–76.

5. *Revista de Occidente,* Año I, No. 2, Segunda época (May 1963), pp. 203–13. This story also appears in Delibes' most recent collection, *La mortaja* (edition cited in Note 1 above), pp. 83–98.

6. *Cuadernos hispanoamericanos,* No. 168 (December, 1963), pp. 562–70. Reprinted in *La mortaja* (edition cited above), pp. 143–61, the text used in this study. Like "El amor propio..." written in

approximately the same period, this tale appears superficially to deal with hunting, but on a deeper level is concerned with human relationships, man's lack of feeling for his fellows, and thus both spring from the same basic thematic and creative impulses as *Las ratas*.

7. Barcelona: Ediciones G. P., undated. (Library stamp "June 1959" indicates publication prior to that date).

8. Since completion of the original draft of this study, some of these tales were, in fact, reprinted with others previously unpublished. The collection is treated at the end of this chapter.

9. Barcelona: Destino, 1957. Despite an implicit recognition of excellence in the Royal Spanish Academy's award of its Fastenrath Prize, this collection remains essentially unstudied, and received only scattered reviews.

10. This is also the title of Delibes' most recent collection. The tale here discussed is reprinted as the first and longest of nine narratives, and gives its title to the entire collection. Some critics have considered "The Shroud" one of Delibes' best and most typical pieces of fiction, which may in part account for its reprinting and the choice of title, which otherwise is difficult to explain—its application to the remaining stories in the volume would be symbolic, perhaps referring to the "shrouding" facade or lack of authenticity found in many of the characters and situations.

11. Miguel Angel Pastor, in his prologue cited in Note 1 above, suggests that "El Senderines" represents a stage of childhood midway between Daniel in *El camino* and El Nini in *Las ratas*, something of a variation on the suggestion in this chapter that "El Senderines" and his father anticipate aspects of "El Nini" and tío Ratero.

Chapter Six

1. *Complete Works* (Barcelona: Destino, 1966), p. 12.

2. *Loc. cit.*

3. *Ibid.*, p. 13.

4. Barcelona: Destino, 1955.

5. Francisco Casanova, "El libro del año," in *Gaceta Regional* (Salamanca), January 1, 1958.

6. This untranslatable concept denotes a typically Spanish institution, a group with some common interest which meets on a regular basis over an extended period.

7. Barcelona: Destino, 1958.

Chapter Seven

1. Miguel Delibes, *Por esos mundos* (Barcelona: Destino, 1961), p. 7.

2. *Ibid.*, p. 8.
3. *Loc. cit.*
4. Madrid: Editora Nacional, 1956.
5. *Por esos mundos*, p. 25.
6. The work is *La Araucana*, by Alonso de Ercilla.
7. Madrid: Ediciones Cid, 1963.
8. Barcelona: Destino, 1966.
9. Madrid: Alianza Editorial, 1968.

Chapter Eight

1. These dramatic possibilities were recognized by José María de Quinto, who planned a stage version of *La hoja roja.*
2. Barcelona: Destino, 1959.
3. Barcelona: Destino, 1968.
4. *Ibid.*, p. 9.
5. *Ibid.*, p. 11.
6. José Julio Perlado, "Miguel Delibes: *La hoja roja,*" in *La estafeta literaria* (Madrid), October 10, 1959.
7. *"La hoja roja* por Miguel Delibes," in *ABC* (Madrid), March 6, 1960.
8. "La vida de los libros," *Destino* (Barcelona), July 18, 1959.
9. Padre Martín Descalzo, "Cosas de Dios," *El norte de Castilla* (Valladolid), June 26, 1960.
10. *"La hoja roja* de Miguel Delibes," in *Destino* (Barcelona), October 3, 1959.

Chapter Nine

1. *La caza de la perdiz roja* was originally published as a separate volume in a limited edition, relatively expensive because of its quantity of photographs and sketches, and elegant format on heavy grey paper with red ink (Barcelona: Lumen, 1962, 1963). These refinements are lacking in the *Obra completa* edition, Volume Two (Barcelona: Destino, 1966).
2. Barcelona: Destino, 1965.
3. Barcelona: Destino, 1968.
4. *Ibid.*, p. 157.
5. *Ibid.*, p. 158.
6. Barcelona: Lumen, 1964.
7. Barcelona, 1964. No copy was available for my examination; the original publisher was Noguer. The limited edition of 150 copies

contained engravings by the Catalan artist Jaume Plá and a prologue by Pedro Laín Entralgo (lacking in *Obra completa*).

8. Manual García Viñó, *Novela española actual* (Madrid: Guadarrama, 1967), p. 32. This is the theme of a chapter, "Reacción ante el progreso," in which García Viñó affirms that Delibes believes that all products of technology, all inventions of man are "something false and dangerous for [man's]true essence." While the reasons for the critic's hostility are not entirely clear, García Viñó's dislike of Delibes is such that when unable to deny his importance among living Spanish novelists, he prefers to say that his relative rank means little, as contemporary Spanish literature offers no competition.

Chapter Ten

1. Antonio Vilanova, *"Las ratas* de Miguel Delibes, Premio de la Crítica, 1962," *Destino* (Barcelona), April 27, 1963.
2. "Castilla negra y Castilla blanca," originally published in *La vanguardia* (Barcelona), July 24, 1964; reprinted in *Vivir al día* (Barcelona: Destino, 1968), pp. 177–80.
3. "Los pueblos moribundos," originally published in *El norte de Castilla* (Valladolid), 1961; reprinted in *Vivir al día*, pp. 114–16.
4. Barcelona: Destino, 1962.
5. *"La ruina de Castilla,"* reprinted in *Vivir al día*, pp. 174–76.
6. "Entrevista con Miguel Delibes," *Madrid*, August 9, 1962.
7. "La cara lavada," originally published in *El norte de Castilla,* 1960; reprinted in *Vivir al día*, pp. 111–13.
8. "Veinticuatro horas con Miguel Delibes," *La Prensa (Barcelona)*, June 5, 1965.
9. R. Vázquez Zamora, "Miguel Delibes: *Las ratas,"* *Destino* (Barcelona), May 19, 1962.
10. Francisco Umbral, " Miguel Delibes: *Las ratas,"* *Punta Europa* (June, 1962), pp. 117–18.
11. Vázquez Zamora, *op. cit.*, p. 16.
12. A Valencia, "Sociología, tremendismo, estilo," *Madrid*, May 3, 1962.
13. J. L. Sampedro, "Delibes, Miguel. *Las ratas,"* *Revista de Occidente*, Serie 2, Vol. II, No. 6, 382–85.
14. M. García Viñó, *Novela española actual* (Madrid: Guadarrama, 1967), p. 24.
15. For example, Enrique Sordo, "Los cazadores de ratas," *Solidaridad Nacional* (Barcelona), May 2, 1963.
16. Vilanova, *loc. cit.*
17. *Ibid.*

Chapter Eleven

1. Barcelona: Destino, 1966.

2. María Luisa Bombal, *La amortajada* (Santiago: Nascimiento, 1941).

3. Elena Quiroga, *Algo pasa en la calle* (Barcelona: Destino, 1954). The similarities between this novel and *Cinco horas con Mario* have been studied, although only partially, in an article by Obdulia Guerrero, "Miguel Delibes y su novela *Cinco horas con Mario*," in *Cuadernos Hispanoamericanos*, LXX, No. 210, 614–21.

4. *Cinco horas con Mario*, pp. 282–83.

Chapter Twelve

1. Barcelona: Destino, 1969. Hereinafter referred to as *Parable*.

2. *Vivir al día* (Barcelona: Destino, 1968), p. 158; cited in Chapter 8.

3. *La estafeta literaria* (Madrid), March 22, 1965.

4. Jośe Corrales Egea, "Situación actual de la novela española: La 'contraola'," Supplement to *Insula*, No. 282 (May, 1970), p. 24.

5. The name "Don Abdón" is interesting, obviously an invention of Delibes with symbolic connotations, for no such name exists in Spanish. Not only does it read the same forward and backward, but one element contradicts the other. "Don," in addition to its use as a title, can signify a gift, while "Abdón" would mean its revocation, something similar to "he who gives and takes away" (and perhaps intended to evoke the biblical connotation, since Don Abdón has many godlike attributes). Obviously, it is also intended to insinuate the farcical nature of governments, secular and ecclesiastical.

Selected Bibliography

Primary Sources

The Writings of Miguel Delibes

With few exceptions, only major works are listed, omitting the numerous newspaper and critical articles which have appeared during nearly a quarter-century. Some of these have been collected in volume form, others will presumably be published in the *Obra completa* (or consigned to oblivion by their author), so that only especially significant articles and short stories published individually are listed.

1. *Collections*

Mi mundo y el mundo (Valladolid: Editorial Miñon, 1969). Selections from the novels and travel works. particularly chosen for appropriateness for use with school children.

Obra completa (Barcelona: Destino, 1964, 1966, 1968), Vols. I, II, III. This collection, still in process of publication, contains (I) *La sombra del ciprés es alargada, El camino, Mi idolatrado hijo Sisí;* (II) the two *Diaries* of Lorenzo, the books on hunting, and *Viejas historias de Castilla la Vieja;* (III) *Aún es de día, La hoja roja,* and *Las ratas.* Delibes' prologues to these volumes, especially to II and III, are valuable essays in self-criticism and contain useful autobiographical notes.

Vivir al día (Barcelona: Destino, 1968). Selected articles previously published from 1953 to 1967 on a wide variety of topics from literature to soccer.

2. *Books* (novels marked with an asterisk).

*Aún es de día (Barcelona: Destino, 1949).

*El camino (Barcelona: Destino, 1950). There is an edition for American students (New York: Holt, 1960) by José Amor Vázquez and Ruth Kossoff, and one for British students (London: Harrap, 1963) with an English introduction by Phillip Pollack. American translation, *The Path* (New York: John Day Co., 1961; translators John and Brita Haycraft), and an English version published the previous year in London by Hamish Hamilton. Translations to French, Portuguese, and other languages.

Castilla (Barcelona: Noguer, 1964). Limited edition. Same text, but without illustrations, published as *Viejas historias de Castilla la Vieja.*

La caza de la perdiz roja (Barcelona: Lumen, 1963).

*Cinco horas con Mario (Barcelona: Destino, 1966).

Diario de un cazador (Barcelona: Destino, 1955). Premio Nacional de Literatura, 1955.

Europa, parada y fonda (Madrid: Ediciones Cid, 1963).

La hoja roja (Barcelona: Destino, 1959).

El libro de la caza menor (Barcelona: Destino, 1964).

Mi idolatrado hijo Sisí (Barcelona: Destino, 1953).

La mortaja (Madrid: Alianza Editorial, 1970).

Un novelista descubre América (Madrid: Editora Nacional, 1956). Incorporated in *Por esos mundos.*

Parábola del náufrago (Barcelona: Destino, 1969).

La partida (Barcelona: Caralt, 1954).

Por esos mundos (Barcelona: Destino, 1961).

La primavera de Praga (Madrid: Alianza Editorial, 1968).

Las ratas (Barcelona: Destino, 1962). Premio de la Crítica, 1963.

Siestas con viento sur (Barcelona: Destino, 1957). Premio Fastenrath de la Real Academia Española.

La sombra del ciprés es alargada (Barcelona: Destino, 1948). Premio Nadal, 1947.

USA y yo (Barcelona: Destino, 1966).

Viejas historias de Castilla la Vieja (Barcelona: Lumen, 1964).

3. *Articles, lectures, short stories*

"Algo más sobre premios," *El norte de Castilla* (Valladolid), July 21, 1962 (deals with relation of author-publisher).

"El amor propio de Juanito Osuna," *Revista de Occidente,* Año I, No. 2, segunda época (May, 1963) 203–13. One of Delibes' most significant narratives, also reprinted in *La mortaja.*

"Autocrítica de *Mi idolatrado hijo Sisí,*" *Ateneo,* April 1, 1959.

"El autor ante su obra," important unpublished self-criticism, delivered as lecture in 1965.

"El autor enjuicia su obra," *Estafeta literaria,* March 22, 1964.

"La barbería," (short story separately published), portada, Coll (Barcelona: Ed. G P, 1957).

"El conejo," *Cuadernos hispanoamericanos,* No. 168 (Dec., 1963), pp. 562–70 [also in *La mortaja.*]

"Medio siglo de novela española," *Comprendre,* Nos. 17–18 (1957), pp. 242–47.

"La milana," *Mundo hispánico,* Año XVI, No. 182 (May, 1963), pp. 73–76.

"El novelista y sus personajes," unpublished lecture, given various times, 1963–1966.

"Notas sobre la novela española contemporánea," *Cuadernos del congreso por la libertad de la cultura,* No. 63 (1962), pp. 34–38. Also published as "La novela española contemporánea," *Indice,* XVII, 173 (May, 1963), 9–10.

"Panorama de la joven novela española," *Ateneo,* II, 36 (June 6, 1953), 6–7.

"El recuerdo," *Mundo hispánico,* Año II, No. 21 (Dec., 1949), pp. 58–59.

SECONDARY SOURCES

The following selection represents less than ten percent of the material investigated during preparation of this study. Much had to be eliminated because of repetitiveness, political bent, or extreme difficulty of access. Both secondary material in general, and the more complete bibliographies, are almost inaccessible to the general public, found either in Spanish newspaper files, or theses, largely unpublished. The most inclusive bibliography, up to 1964, is found in the doctoral thesis of M. Alvarez Rodríguez, "Vida y obra de Miguel Delibes," University of Salamanca, 1964. There is a bibliography in the work of Leo Hickey, *Cinco horas con Miguel Delibes* (Madrid: Editorial Prensa Española, 1968), dedicated entirely to primary sources and translations thereof, and with no pretentions to completeness. It has some religious bias, but is perhaps the only bibliography of any length of general diffusion.

1. *Books and Theses*

Alvarez Rodríguez, Maximino. "Vida y obra de Miguel Delibes," doctoral thesis, University of Salamanca, 1964. There are other limitations, but the most serious is limited availability, for this is one of the most complete and respectable studies of Delibes' life and works up to and including *Las ratas.* Considerations include novelistic constants, authenticity, *españolismo,* family unity, determinism, materialism versus idealism, nature, death, religion, Delibes on politics and social issues, his concept of the novel, realistic, lyric, humorous, and existential elements, and a novel-by-novel discussion of eight long narratives, as well as a chapter on miscellaneous works.

Gual, Francine. "La vie rustique et la nature dans l'oeuvre de Miguel Delibes" (Diplôme d'études supérieures espagnol, Université de Montpellier, 1963). Studies life and works of Delibes, emphasizing the rustic aspects and nature in the first three novels and two short story collections, as well as one travel book *(Por esos mundos).*

Hickey, Leo. *Cinco horas con Miguel Delibes* (Madrid: Editorial Prensa
Española, 1968). This is an updating and slight revision of a doctoral
thesis, "Miguel Delibes, escritor católico," University of Madrid
(1966), whose title is much more descriptive of the content.
Hickey's biographical section relies heavily upon Alvarez, and most
of the body of the work is devoted to establishing criteria for the
Catholic novel and deciding whether or not Delibes fits. (Except for
Aún es de día, it is decided that he does not). Despite the strong and
perhaps irrelevant emphasis on orthodoxy in Delibes' works, this
critic offers one of the most complete studies to date, and more or
less by accident includes some significant insights tangential to his
major interest.

Link, Judith Ann. "Major Themes in the Novels of Miguel Delibes,"
unpublished M. A. thesis, University of Oklahoma (Norman), 1960.
Surveys themes of the postwar generation, as found in Delibes'
novels, emphasizing the city-country duality and spiritualism versus
materialism. Covers seven novels up to *La hoja roja,* and two short
story collections, deciding that Delibes cannot be classified. Major
themes identified are death, war, pessimism, renunciation of life,
fatalism; it is affirmed that "For Delibes, the city seems to represent
a material, sensual, egotistic and superficial existence . . . a dark,
bustling, dirty entity which has a negative effect on man . . . Man in
modern society is materialistic, greedy, cruel, ambitious, sensual,
frivolous, devoid of spiritual direction." Incorrectly states that
Delibes actually fought in the Civil War and personally witnessed its
horror, supposing a consequent existentialism, but correctly rejects
the attribution of *tremendismo.*

Marín Hernández, María Fuensanta. "La obra de Miguel Delibes," tesis
de Licenciatura, Universidad de Murcia, 1965. Concentrates on
treatment of children and feminine characters, the theme of
solitude, attitudes toward death, the vision of nature, provincial life,
and the hunt.

Plaza Camarero, Faustino. "El niño en la obra de Miguel Delibes," tesis
de Licenciatura, Universidad de La Laguna, 1961. The author is a
teacher in the order of Christian Brothers (La Salle), who in part
chose Delibes as a subject since the novelist received much of his
schooling from this order. There is an introductory section devoted
to the child, his world and psychology, and treatment of these in
more generalized literature, and then a narrowing of the focus to
Delibes, considering the child in his works as (1) a subject of

education; (2) examples of sad or unfortunate childhoods; (3) the child as victim; (4) the child as accomplice; (5) innocence; and (6) "grown-up children."

Soladana Carro, Amaro. "Lo religioso en la obra novelística de Miguel Delibes," tesis de Licenciatura, Universidad de Salamanca, 1965. This work first established criteria for defining the "religious novel" (the author is a friar), but in terms which do not essentially separate this genre from the novel of religious problems, ethics, or metaphysics. While initially giving prime importance to the concept of human responsibility, the treatment evolves from a broad and general idea of the "religious novel" to a point where concrete characters and situations are judged according to traditional dogma.

2. *Articles and Sections in Longer Works*

Alborg, J. L. *Hora actual de la novela española* (Madrid: Taurus 1958), pp. 153–65. Delibes is one of eight novelists included in this first volume (Part I of a series). His works are studied only up to the *Diary,* and tend to emphasize the first three or four. Notable largely for coining the phrases *historia de un pesimismo* and *historia de un optimismo* to refer to the first two novels, respectively.

Amor Vázquez, José and Kossoff, Ruth. Introduction to the Holt scholastic edition of *El camino* (1960). Gives brief biography and reviews works up to the *Diario de un cazador,* not extensively, but with good insights. In English and should be widely available.

Bellini, Giuseppe. Introduction to *Siesta con vento sud* (Milan: Nuova Accademia Editrice, 1959). Observations by the translator-editor call attention particularly to the use of conversational tone, the style of everyday speech, the humble nature of Delibes' protagonists, and provides a competent, schematic review of the novelist's life and works up to that date.

Caballero Bonald, J. M. "La integridad narrativa de Miguel Delibes." *Papeles de Son Armadans,* VI, No. 17 (August, 1957), 209–22. Written by one of a previously rather hostile faction, the article is very favorable to Delibes, referring to his *"honradez expresiva . . . limpieza ornamental, la sobria y a la vez exuberante categoría de pureza lingüistica, la maestría narrativa . . ."*

Cano, José Luis. "Los libros del mes," *Insula* (June, 1948). One of the first appreciations of values implicit in Delibes' earliest novel, this critic has many subsequent reviews, nearly all helpful, in the same literary organ: *"Aun es de día," Insula,* V, 49 (January, 1950); *"El camino," Insula,* VI, 63 (March, 1951); *"Diario de un cazador,"*

Insula, X, 114 (June, 1955); *"Mi idolatrado hijo Sisí," Insula,* IX, 97 (January, 1954); *"La sombra del ciprés es alargada," Insula,* III, 30 (June, 1948).

Castellet, José María. "La joven novela española," *Sur,* No. 284 (September–October 1963), pp. 49–51. Helps to situate Delibes in total perspective of postwar novel, citing him as best known (with Cela) of representatives of *realismo crítico.*

Coindreau, Maurice E. Preface to *Sisi, Mon Fils Adoré* (Paris: Gallimard, 1958; trans by J. Francis Reille). Imagines the first four works on a curve, where the first two mark one extreme, *El camino* the other, and *My Adored Son Sisí* a midpoint, a compromise between something dangerously near sentimentalism on the one hand and a realism occasionally too crude on the other. A fairly penetrating discussion of the first four novels, with the observation that Cecilio Rubes is some sort of *Babbitt espagnol.*

Corrales Egea, José. "Situación actual de la novela española: 'La contraola'." Suplemento de *Insula,* No. 282, pp. 21–24. Article is largely dedicated to what its author perceives as a reaction against the *novela social* and objectivist currents prevailing in Spain since the mid-fifties, and he cites among his examples Delibes' latest novel, *Parábola del náufrago,* one of very few critical mentions to date of that work.

García Viño, M. *Novela española actual* (Madrid: Guadarrama, 1967), "Miguel Delibes: Entre la primera y la segunda naturaleza," pp. 17–46. Affirms Delibes is considered among the best and most representative of contemporary novelists by most critics, but then proceeds to a negative critique of Delibes' use of language, repetition, the *santoral,* names, and his "minor aesthetic." García prefers *El camino,* and then *Sisí* among Delibes' novels as having less studied styles than later works, which he calls *estampas costumbristas* but hardly works of art, of little psychological value. He especially attacks *Las ratas,* Delibes' "grayest" novel, which is seen as composed of utterly uninteresting anecdotes, mere pretexts for verbal games. For him, Delibes is essentially a caricaturist, lacking tenderness, fundamentally pessimistic. He criticizes what he believes to be Delibes' theories, and accuses him of "absolute scorn for his characters," pretending to prove that the novelist is "authentically opposed to progress," and twisting his work to show a "typically reactionary attitude," lacking in metaphysical preoccupation and characterized by mental provincialism.

Guerrero, Obdulia. "Miguel Delibes y su novela *Cinco horas con Mario,*" *Cuadernos Hispanoamericanos,* LXX, No. 210, 614—21. Notes Delibes' stylistic preoccupations, realism, psychological penetration, and almost magnetophonic transcription of the language used by the widow. The article is primarily a comparison of the novel named with Elena Quiroga's *Algo pasa en la calle.*

Hickey, Leo. "Miguel Delibes and the Cult of the Infra-Man," The New *Vida Hispánica,* Vol. XII, No. 2 (Summer, 1965), 23—27. Affirms that there is no place in Delibes' works for supermen or heroes, while noting importance of the elemental character. According to this article, "Delibes is not an intellectual writer; he handles not ideas but humanity and humanity at its most elemental level. For him, no importance is to be attached to man's great achievements, great human qualities of intellect . . . will or bodies. He is interested . . . not only primarily but exclusively, in those qualities which make men simply men, those virtues which normally are considered as minor: simplicity, innocence bordering on, or arising out of, ignorance, meekness, resignation, forebearance, acceptance of one's lot, patience, simple, unlegalistic justice, love of the countryside and the un-complex pleasures of life."

Iglesias Laguna, A. *Treinta años de novela española (1938-1968)* (Madrid: Editorial Prensa Española, 1969), pp. 273—81. Emphasizes Delibes' process of simplification, purification of style, narrowing of focus, more limited setting and less plot, more clearly delineated (provincial) novelistic world. However, includes mistaken associations with E. Larreta, and accuses Delibes of exaggerated individualism, egolatry, and a mentality tending to ideological abstraction and "Manicheism." He postulates an influence of Nietzsche and considers Delibes primarily a stylist at the expense of other narrative elements. While affirming that Delibes at his best is unrivalled except by Cela and Matute, the essay is full of ambivalence and its final judgment is ambiguous.

Johnson, Ernest A., Jr. "Miguel Delibes, *El camino—*A Way of Life." *Hispania,* Vol. XLVI, No. 4 (December, 1963), 748—52. While extremely brief, and limited to only one work, this is one of the relatively few treatments in English and should be fairly accessible. It offers little beyond plot material and critical commonplaces, but will serve as an introduction to the novel in question.

Martín Descalzo, J. L. "Mundo y estilo de Miguel Delibes," *Libros y discos* (Madrid), No. 2, (September, 1962). This five-page study by a priest includes Delibes' first ten novels (up to and including *Las ratas)*, emphasizing the division in two groups, those with plots and those without, with a parallel division of characters, as those in the elaborately plotted novels are seen as complex, while those in the plotless works are primitive. Notes vividness of environmental description and sense data, Delibes' power of *poetización de lo vulgar,* his use of language, and his presentation of Castilian religiosity. The world of Delibes is seen as that of the average man, neither dramatically good nor evil, where God is "also" present, a perfect sketch of reality. Padre Martín Descalzo states that Castilian faith is like morphine and easily confused with resignation, admitting the sad truth of Delibes' portrayals of mixed superstition and terror together with faith.

Nora, Eugenio G. de. *La novela española contemporánea (1927–1960),* II, ii. (Madrid: Editorial Gredos, 1962), 155–64. While attempting to give a comprehensive picture of Delibes up to the date of writing, the study is of necessity not too penetrating because of its brevity, despite the talents of this critic. Useful particularly for situating Delibes in the panorama of the postwar novel in general, when studied together with others grouped in the same category.

Pollack, Phillip. Introduction to *El camino* (London: Harrap, 1963). Attempts to relate *El camino* to contemporary British fiction, and notes the importance in Delibes' work of "the direction which [the individual] gives his own life." There is a generally competent survey of Delibes' narratives, both novels and short stories, up to *La hoja roja,* and an attempt to derive constant themes, among which the father-son relationship is seen as particularly important. Among the very few general studies in English, this one is to be highly recommended.

Rodríguez Alcalde, L. "El novelista Miguel Delibes," *El libro español,* IX, No. 97 (January, 1966), I.N.L.E., 8–15. A survey of most of the critical commonplaces up to the date of writing, in which he answers and defends Delibes against certain accusations of imitation, "grayness," and excess "Naturalism." Fairly objective evaluation of virtues and defects of the individual novels up to *La hoja roja.*

Sampedro, José Luis. "Delibes, Miguel. *Las ratas,"* *Revista de Occidente,* Serie 2, Vol. II, No. 6, 382–85. A highly intelligent critic and novelist, writing in one of Spain's most respected literary periodicals, gives one of the best interpretations of a key work by Delibes.

Umbral, Francisco. "Miguel Delibes en la novela tradicional," *Punta Europa*, Nos. 57–58 (Sept.-Oct., 1960), pp. 29–35. A survey of novels up to *La hoja roja*, in which certain comparisons are suggested, but not fully developed, including a possibly interesting glimpse of a resemblance between a portion of the work of Delibes and that of Sánchez-Ferlosio.

INDEX

83596